PRAYING

The League of Prayer

(1891-2011)

Compiled and edited

by

Norman Armistead

British Library Cataloguing in Publication Data.
A catalogue record for this book is available
from the British Library.

ISBN 978 086071 651 8

*Praying always with all prayer and supplication in the Spirit,
being watchful to this end with all perseverance and
supplication for all saints …(Ephesians 8: 18, NKJV)*

Commissioned Publication of

23 Park Road, Ilkeston, Derbyshire DE7 5DA
Tel: 0115 932 0643 ● www.moorleys.co.uk

Major Norman Armistead is a retired Salvation Army Officer. He has served as Director of the League of Prayer and is the current editor of *The Flame* magazine.

Bible verses in Part Two are taken from the *New King James Version.*

Cover logo by Jim Moss.

Frontispiece: Richard Reader Harris, QC.

Contents

Photo W. S. Stuart.   Richmond

Reader Harris.

iv

PREFACE

As the psalmist reminds us, a thousand years in the eyes of the Lord are like yesterday when it is past. Later on, in Psalm 90, we are encouraged to use wisely the time that we have. Only eternity will reveal the full impact of the one hundred and twenty years ministry of the League of Prayer (1891-2011).

As I was preparing this book, it dawned on me that my memory of the League goes back at least thirty years to some times of rich fellowship and inspiring gatherings, notably at the Hayes Conference, Swanwick, Derbyshire, when the message of full salvation was preached by men of God under the powerful anointing of the Holy Spirit. Readers will have their own precious memories of blessing received through the ministry of the League of Prayer.

This book is published to commemorate this movement, which played such a formative role in the development of the British Holiness movement. It stands in the Wesleyan tradition in its emphasis on the call to full salvation. Its stress on scriptural holiness follows John Wesley's teaching that the Christian's heart could be cleansed from all sin, an experience received by faith, and to which the Holy Spirit bears witness. There are a number of terms used to describe this experience. Those used in this book, in the main, are 'the Baptism with the Holy Spirit' and 'sanctification'. Others include 'the second blessing', 'perfect love' and 'the blessing of a clean heart'.

Part One is a brief historical sketch of the League, which also introduces Richard Reader Harris, QC (1847-1909), an Anglican layman and prominent English barrister, who trained for the bar in 1883 and was called at Gray's Inn, where he was elected to the Bench. He founded the League of Prayer (formerly the Pentecostal League of Prayer) in 1891, in Battersea, London, out of a deep concern for the spiritual life of the church. His vision was of an interdenominational movement of dedicated Christian men and women who would commit themselves to pray regularly for (1) the infilling of the Holy Spirit for all believers, (2) revival of the churches, and (3) the spread of scriptural holiness. The following pages will give some indication as to how this developed.

Part Two comprises devotional readings taken from the League of Prayer newsletters and the pens of Reader Harris, Oswald Chambers, Percy Hassam, and others, and will give a flavour of the League's message as it has been delivered – in print and in preaching – over the course of its history. May it also lead to our renewed dedication to the task of reaching today's generation with the message of full salvation in the time that we have available. – NA.

FOREWORD

The late nineteenth century and the dawn of the twentieth saw the founding of several holiness movements, including Cliff College (1884), the Faith Mission (1886), Japan Evangelistic Band (1903), Oriental Missionary Society (1905), and the International Holiness Mission (1907). The League of Prayer – formerly the Pentecostal League of Prayer – came into being, in 1891, through the vision of Richard Reader Harris, QC, an Anglican layman, who was deeply impressed by the spiritual needs of the church and the world. The movement began as, and remained, an interdenominational prayer movement which linked Christians who shared a concern for a true outpouring of the Holy Spirit and who believed that entire sanctification was the birthright of every believer.

Reader Harris and his wife, Mary, had claimed and received the sanctifying fullness of the Holy Spirit and, as a consequence, hundreds of others were blessed in a similar manner. His mission, Speke Hall, Battersea, London, became a powerhouse from which great blessing spread to other places as Reader Harris preached full salvation to packed congregations.

Throughout the one hundred and twenty years of its existence the League has continued to bring together Christians of all churches who have met regularly in prayer groups and in larger gatherings in this country and abroad. Its threefold aim which first inspired Reader Harris remained the vision of the movement through the years: the infilling of the Holy Spirit for all believers; revival in the churches; and the spread of scriptural holiness in the life of every believer.

Now in the twenty-first century, many Christians are equally concerned both about the spiritual condition of the churches and of the nation. The spiritual and moral climate is such that only a real move of God in reviving power can change the situation, and only prayer can bring revival in our day. There is no other way, and to look for it in any other direction is to ignore the clear teaching of Scripture. In a dark day when the people of God were demoralised, the prophet Ezekiel spoke of God seeking 'a man to stand in the gap' to stem the tide of national ruin.

It is a sad but realistic fact that the real gap in the church today is in the ranks of the intercessors – those who recognise the priority of prayer and are committed to it. There is also a gap in the ranks of those who stand courageously for biblical standards of holy living. Lifestyles may change, but God's moral standards do not change. Whilst after one hundred and twenty years it is felt that the League of Prayer as a movement has completed its ministry, its three-fold prayer thrust remains as urgent as ever.

With this commemorative book the call goes out for more intercessors to plead at the throne of grace for God's intervention in these critical days.

Leslie Evans
Former General Director/Secretary of the League of Prayer
and current Chairman of the Council

ACKNOWLEDGEMENTS

This book, which celebrates the ministry of the League of Prayer (1891-2011), a movement founded by Richard Reader Harris, QC, an Anglican layman, in 1891, is made possible only through the generous support of a number of people. First and foremost I am grateful for access to the Rev Geoffrey N. Fewkes' dissertation on Reader Harris and the Pentecostal League of Prayer, submitted in partial fulfilment of the requirements of the Victoria University of Manchester, for the degree of Master of Arts in Theology. All who have read this masterly piece of research will immediately recognise its influence on this book. I am indebted to Geoffrey Fewkes and offer him my sincere thanks for his estimable contribution to this project.

I am also indebted to others who have kindly read the manuscript and made helpful comments. Prominent among these is the Rev Leslie Evans, the last General Director and Secretary of the League of Prayer, whose observations have in particular helped to elucidate some of the theological passages. He has also provided the foreword to the book. The Rev Dr Denis Applebee who has been a great encourager to me over many years suggested the sub headings. I am also grateful to the Rev Dr Peter W. Gentry whose fellowship and support, particularly with *The Flame* magazine, remains a constant source of inspiration, for kindly reading the manuscript and making helpful comments. The Rev Paul M. James, an Anglican clergyman and son of the Rev Maynard G. James, has also read the manuscript.

There are others who have made valuable contributions to this project. The Rev Douglas A. Crossman searched his attic to find literature by Reader Harris, and extracts have found their way into this book. I thank Alistair Barclay and his late wife, Valerie, for their unfailing support. Part Two of the book comprises passages from the rich treasury of writings that have enriched the pages of the League of Prayer newsletters over many years, as well as material from Reader Harris, Oswald Chambers and others who have served within the League. Other contributors are the Rev Leslie Evans, Miss Joyce Gautrey, Mr David Foot Nash, Mr J. Albert Harper, the Rev Percy Hassam, Majors Allister Smith, Derek Dolling and Norman Armistead. In addition to many of the above, I have also had access to the minutes of the council of the League of Prayer, books by Reader Harris and www.calvaryholinessmission.org.

The book belongs to the above and to League members, present and in the past, whose influence in prayer and service cannot be measured, but will one day be revealed by the One who entered this world to seek and to save the lost, and who will one day return to claim His own.

Any deficiencies in the text are entirely my own.

Norman Armistead
Major

CONTRIBUTORS

Reader Harris (RH)

Leslie Evans (LE)

Allister Smith (AS)

David Foot Nash (DFN)

Oswald Chambers (OC)

Percy Hassam (PH)

J. Albert Harper (JAH)

Joyce Gautrey (JG)

Derek Dolling (DD)

Norman Armistead (NA)

PART ONE

Historical

The League of Prayer

(1891-2011)

The League of Prayer

Reader Harris

The Pentecostal League of Prayer was the vision of a larger-than-life adventurer and traveller, an engineer then lawyer by profession, who was deeply concerned for the spiritual life of the churches and the wider needs of the community, especially the poor. His compelling desire was to awaken Christians to the need to relate their faith effectively to the changing world around them, to be the salt and light, of which Jesus speaks (Matthew 5: 13-16). He set out to establish an inter-church fellowship committed to prayer with a threefold objective; that is, it was born out of a strong desire to see, firstly, Christian believers filled with the Holy Spirit and, secondly, to be engaged in earnest prayer for the revival of the churches. Thirdly, its *raison d'etre* was the promotion of the Wesleyan doctrine of scriptural holiness as a necessary and vital experience for all believers. Members agreed to pray regularly for these three objectives.

Richard Reader Harris, the founder, was born at Worcester on 5 July 1847. He left school early due to a breakdown in family fortunes and started work with the Great Western Railway, continuing his studies at night. At the age of twenty-one, he was appointed one of the Constructing Engineers on the Metropolitan extension of the Great Eastern Railway, and moved to London. But five years before moving to London, at sixteen years of age, a notable event took place in his life that seems to have marked an early stage in his spiritual journey. Harris took along his mother's Bible when attending confirmation classes and asked the vicar if the commands of the Sermon on the Mount were binding upon man and the promises binding upon God. Significantly, in view of what was to follow in later years, the particular verse in question was: "Be ye therefore perfect, even as your Father which is in heaven is perfect" (Matthew 5: 48). At the time he accepted the answer he received at its face value, but later it raised disturbing questions, and as time passed, it seemed to him that religious leaders did not take God at His word, for in response to his question he was told that the Sermon on the Mount was an expression of aims and ideals that Christians may seek, but which in this life they cannot hope to reach.

In spite of this he remained committed to the pursuit of these ideals and maintained a strong desire to see them practised in daily life, but initially sought answers in the wrong place. When he moved to London to take up his post with the Great Eastern Railway, his continued search brought him under the influence of Charles Bradlaugh (1833-1891), freethinker and political activist, and founder of the National Secular Society. Still looking for answers, he attended Bradlaugh's meetings at the Hall of Science, and before long embraced agnosticism and joined the Ethical Society. He became a total abstainer, non-smoker and one of Bradlaugh's lecturers.

He was with the Great Eastern Railway for four years before travelling to Bolivia in March 1893 as Engineer-in-Chief for the Bolivian Government. In Bolivia, Harris experienced an earthquake, yellow fever, revolution, and even a death sentence, but, sadly, still *"without any serious thought of God"*. Then another significant incident took place, which should have alerted him to the intervention of divine providence. When his mother became seriously ill he took six months leave of absence to be with her. Unfortunately after a hair-raising journey, he missed the steamer by six hours and had to wait another two weeks for the next one. Later on he admitted that every day during those two weeks he had cursed God. But when the boat arrived he discovered that the one he had missed had sunk with all hands. The few passengers were drowned while sleeping. And that was the steamer he cursed God for missing!

Crucial Turning Point

Clearly the hand of God was upon him, though the significance of that deliverance appears to have been lost on him at the time. Then, when he was appointed as Bolivia's Financial Commissioner for Europe, based in London, his work brought him into contact with John G. Bristow, senior partner with the legal firm, Wilson, Bristow and Carpmael. This association proved to be a crucial turning point in Harris's spiritual pilgrimage. He met John Bristow's daughter, Mary, who became his spiritual mentor first, before becoming his wife. Mary was a Congregationalist with strong convictions who directed his Bible reading and instructed him in the way of salvation till in due course he came to faith. They were married on 10 August 1880.

His tract *Four-Fold Salvation*, which was foundational in the teaching of the League of Prayer, and the nearest we have to 'a theology of experience' published by him, reflects his own personal experience and was widely distributed throughout the League centres until comparatively recent days. In the tract Harris taught that the new birth followed conversion and salvation was completed with the baptism in the Holy Spirit and ongoing growth in grace. The work of conversion is always initiated by the grace of God. John Wesley believed that God's prevenient grace was intended to be for all people. He said: "The grace or love of God, whence cometh our salvation, is *free in all* and *free for all.*" The need for this prevenient grace, that is the grace of God that goes before or precedes any movement of man towards God, is based on humanity's fallen condition. In fact, the command to repent and believe, found throughout Scripture, would be impossible were it not for the grace of God.

It may well be that Reader Harris's legal training led to a too rigid definition of conversion and regeneration. Most evangelicals today would equate the two. However, for Harris, it was without a doubt God's preliminary or prevenient grace that had brought Mary into his life and it was her influence that led him in the direction of the Church. It was there at St James, Clapham Park, that he met the Rev Aubrey Price, and joined the church prayer group. Having been called to the Bar at Grey's Inn on 16 November 1883, he also joined the Lawyers' Prayer Union. But this did not satisfy his persistent soul hunger. There was a growing conviction of the need for a real spiritual experience. In his tract, he described this phase as being converted but not born again.

It was whilst on a train journey from Paddington to Ealing that Reader Harris read *Union With Christ* by Handley Moule, a frequent speaker at the Keswick Convention, and his eyes were opened to the true nature of regeneration. There and then he prayed and accepted by faith the Holy Spirit and received a distinct witness that he was born again, born of God.

Speke Hall

Soon after his new birth experience, with a deep desire to reach the lost for Christ, ever the activist, he hired Speke Hall, a mission hall in Battersea, filling its 1,400 seats every Sunday evening. He was an inspirational speaker and charismatic figure, able to relate to ordinary men and women. His speaking was direct and practical, laced with humour. Reader Harris and his wife saw these people as their life mission, not only offering the gospel, but like the infant Salvation Army at the time, practical support as well. A contemporary letter heading of the Pentecostal League stated that its mission was 'the filling of the Holy Spirit for all believers, the revival of the churches, and *the salvation of the masses.*'

Four-Fold Salvation

The nineteenth century saw the rise of the Holiness Movement in the United States and a number of prominent leaders visited the United Kingdom. In 1889, Reader Harris invited American holiness evangelists, Dr G.D. Watson and the Rev Frank Sanford, to conduct a mission at Speke Hall, which was increasingly being used as a conference centre and convenient venue for visiting speakers. Their uncompromising call to Christian holiness led to Harris and his wife seeking and finding the fullness of the Holy Spirit for holiness and power. The mission established Speke Hall as a popular London centre for evangelistic missions with a holiness emphasis. About fifty years ago it became a Nazarene church, albeit in new premises.

Reader Harris became a leading advocate of the Holiness Movement, and a key figure in the early days of the movement in the United Kingdom. He was convinced that the experience of entire sanctification was the great need of all believers; the necessity of deliverance from inward as well as outward sin. A pure, clean vessel was vital for effective Christian service. Indeed, the distinctive identity of the League of Prayer as an interdenominational movement depended on its definition of the Pentecostal experience. In *Four-Fold Salvation,* he wrote: "Holiness is character. God will come into our hearts and change our characters. He will make us 'partakers of the divine nature', baptising us with the Holy Ghost, cleansing, filling and empowering our lives. That is perfect salvation." He travelled the land with this message, often as the principal speaker in missions and conventions. The growing work of Speke Hall led to mission halls being opened in and around London with Reader Harris still insisting that his ministry would continue as a mission to the churches. But a firm decision had to be made as to the way forward for the work. On their way back from the first Star Hall Convention,

Manchester, Reader and Mary discussed the issue with Dr Frank Millar. Was it God's will for them to continue opening mission halls for the revived Christians or should they be urged to stay in their churches to bring revival there?

Without question Reader Harris's vision went far beyond Battersea to reach the churches throughout the land and across the seas. The conviction grew that the most effective way of saving the world was through the sanctification of believers. He asked his friends to pray about the matter and it is reported that Harris said: "At the end of the month the Pentecostal League was formed." The year was 1891. The first meeting of the League Council was held in April 1894. The Pentecostal League was a natural extension of the work of Speke Hall, which became the headquarters of the League. Its message touched a raw nerve and met a felt need of the thousands of Christians who became devoted members. In Reader Harris they had a spokesman of commanding presence who combined spirituality with authority, a preacher who was out to convince and enlist. His conferences drew crowds and his publications attracted readers by the thousands.

From the earliest days League members were encouraged to form centres of (say) twelve members to hold a weekly holiness and prayer meeting. The League was essentially, though not exclusively, a lay movement with local secretaries leading the work. Female members wore a bonnet, rather like female members of The Salvation Army. Large numbers gathered for the League's Annual Meeting in Exeter Hall, London, with Harris's organisational skills facilitating transport arrangements across the country. Some 3,000 attended from all denominations. Later the Annual Meeting was held at Kingsway Hall and Caxton Hall, with such notable speakers as the Rev J. Sidlow Baxter and Dr Dinsdale Young.

The League did arouse some opposition even though it was never the intention to divide congregations. It must be admitted, however, with regard to Holy Communion, that Reader Harris, an Anglican layman, did, despite Episcopal protest, administer the sacrament. For Reader Harris also, the baptism with the Spirit was more important than water baptism. These emphases, as has been said, were not intended to be divisive. On the contrary, the Pentecostal League's stress on prayer and holiness, as of first importance, was a call to unity. Harris regretted that the institutional churches, in his view, largely neglected these vital matters.

Welsh Revival

The League's involvement in local mission was both an early expression of Christian unity as well as being an evangelistic outreach. David Thomas (1860-1930), a Welshman from Carmarthen was a prominent accredited missioner with the League. He came to London and opened a drapery business in Falcon Road, Battersea. After joining the League he was subsequently baptized with the Holy Spirit in Speke Hall under the ministry of Dr G.D. Watson. Now wholly set apart for the service of God, his shop became a centre of evangelistic activity and it is said that in every purchase, a tract outlining the way of salvation was enclosed.

David Thomas heard God's call to full-time evangelism and was soon in the forefront of the work at Speke Hall, becoming Harris's right-hand man, sharing Harris's entrepreneurial spirit. Accredited mission band workers, men and women, led missions all over the country. Thomas was to lead a mission in his hometown in the autumn of 1903, followed by another at the invitation of the Free Church Council in January 1904, which was to involve Harris on the closing two days. Both these missions were to make a significant contribution to the factors which prepared the way for the 1904 Welsh Revival. At this point, it may be appropriate to say that one of the leading early workers was Oswald Chambers who regularly preached and wrote for the League. When the League opened its Bible College on Clapham Common, he became the first principal. His untimely death from peritonitis robbed Harris of the one he saw as his successor. Today the continuing popularity of his books which were lovingly and prayerfully edited by his widow may be surprising, especially at a time when the holiness message is not by any means as prominent as once it was.

Divergence of Views

It has been said: "if we would but observe unity in essentials, liberty in non-essentials, charity in all things, our affairs would certainly be in the best possible situation" (Robert Maldenius). It is a sentiment that Reader

Harris would endorse. In his desire to see Christians unite in prayer for revival and holiness, he believed that "time would be saved if we sought and pressed the points of agreement, and above all upon which true Christians must be agreed – the desire to be like Christ in thought, word and deed." In an interview with the Rev S. Horton and quoted by Mary Hooker in her biography of her father, Harris stated: "The movement itself seems fraught with mighty possibilities to the Church of God. There is a great need for emphasis to be laid on the fact that believers can be filled with the Spirit, and that it is only as they are filled that they can render effective service. The Pentecostal League unites all who love Christ in one great praying, expecting and realising brotherhood."

It is sad therefore that a significant disagreement between David Thomas and Reader Harris led to a parting of the ways for the two men. This divergence of views was not over doctrine. It was more to do with strategy. Both wanted to see believers filled with the Holy Spirit and wholly set apart for the service of the Kingdom. Thomas completely agreed with and continued to teach the doctrine of Christian holiness taught by Harris and retained a great respect for him. But after working with the League for fifteen years, he came to the conclusion that Harris's decision, after his conversation with Dr Frank Millar, to continue the interdenominational approach was wrong. He disagreed with this policy after witnessing the apparent discouragement and loss of a number of League members. Whilst Harris had committed the League to inter-church work, Thomas believed with equal conviction that the numbers of people led into the Blessing through his ministry needed to be nurtured in churches definitely committed to the teaching. He now felt compelled to set up new mission halls up and down the country where the teaching of the holiness movement could be preached without contradiction. Both Mary and Reader Harris pleaded with the Thomas and his wife not to leave the League. But Harris could see that his colleague was under considerable strain, and so said: "Thomas, I will set you free if you still feel the Lord is calling you to work outside the churches. Whatever you decide to do in after years, never say I hindered you from doing the will of God."

Authority of Scripture

So with Harris's blessing Thomas withdrew from the League in order to set up the Holiness Mission, later the International Holiness Mission (IHM), based in Sydney Hall, Battersea, in 1907. During the ensuing thirty years the IHM grew into some thirty-three local churches, some centres previously associated with the Pentecostal League joining the new denomination, and also opened a strong overseas work in South Africa. J.D. Drysdale shared similar views to those of David Thomas. He had worked for the League in Ardrossan for some six years but could not continue because he also disagreed with Harris's approach. He later began not only the Emmanuel Bible College at Birkenhead but also the Emmanuel churches on the Wirral. Dr Denis Applebee, well-known in Holiness circles at home and in the States, began his ministry in Emmanuel, and went on to become International Pastor for the World Gospel Mission.

Perhaps it was inevitable that with two strong personalities at the head of the movement those differences of opinion on strategy and promoting the experience would arise. The League was never throughout its history a church; it was always a union of like-minded and similarly experienced men and women whose mission was to try to be a leaven within the churches and beyond in the world. Throughout its one hundred and twenty years history, it has remained committed to this message of full salvation.

Reader Harris was not an academically trained theologian yet he was a fearless advocate of the Christian perfection as taught by Wesley. His message stressed that the whole of our human nature has been affected by sin and that Christ secured complete deliverance from sin on the Cross. Repentance and conversion, and regeneration, as Harris saw it, were the two sides of the same coin, the one a human and the other a divine activity. Both were essential to be saved. Christ, he said, is the Saviour from *all* sin. God in Christ has made provision for complete deliverance and it was to the authority of Scripture that he appealed. From the Bible he pointed to the Cross as a sufficient remedy for the sin problem. Every experience had to be supported by an appeal to the Scriptures and to the Cross. Reader and Mary Harris preached a pre-millennial return of Christ and His reign on earth, which lent urgency to their message.

The Pivotal Influence of The League

The early years of the twentieth century not only saw the halcyon days of the Holiness Movement, but also the rise of the Pentecostal churches with their stress on the gifts of the Spirit, particularly speaking in tongues with the claim that the gift of tongues was the ultimate evidence of the baptism with the Spirit, a view that was at variance with the teaching of the Holiness movement. Harris did not deny that tongues was a gift from God, but carefully taught that the gifts of the Spirit are not to be confused with the graces of the Spirit.

One man who sought to be a reconciling influence between the two groups became the IHM's foremost evangelist. Maynard G. James, another fiery Welshman, from the Holiness Mission in Bargoed, had trained at Cliff College in the closing years of Samuel Chadwick's time as principal, before joining IHM. Probably inspired by George Jeffreys, founder of the Elim Pentecostal Church [Elim Foursquare Gospel], whose crusades were sweeping the country at the time, James included divine healing in his ministry and was supportive of speaking in tongues though he never spoke in tongues himself and did not regard it as the conclusive evidence of the baptism with the Spirit. Speaking in tongues, he believed, was not a major gift but, as God had given it, it should not be despised. This stance brought him into conflict with the IHM Council, who took a decidedly different view on these matters and led to James, along with Jack Ford, Leonard Ravenhill and Clifford Filer withdrawing to form the Calvary Holiness Church, in1934, which grew to about the same size as the IHM.

It must not be construed that the story of the Holiness Movement in Britain, and, as readers will no doubt have noted, the League of Prayer's pivotal influence within it, is predominantly a tale of division between the groups. Vigorous debate among strong personalities did lead to the parting of the ways but not to a loss of respect or a dilution of the essential teaching that was central to the holiness message. A deep fraternal relationship between leaders and members remained. Leaders of all holiness groups frequently shared the same platform at convention gatherings, not least for the League of Prayer. Both the Calvary Holiness Church and the International Holiness Mission continued until the early 1950s, when in the changing circumstances of the post-war era both groups saw decline, and they both found a new home in the Church of the

11

Nazarene. The League of Prayer also declined during the Second World War but was revived in 1947 through the vision, inspiration and energy of the Rev Percy Hassam who served as General Secretary until his Home Call in 1965. J. Albert Harper who thus fulfilled an early conviction that his main ministry as a Christian worker was to be through the League of Prayer succeeded him. He had previously trained at Cliff College and had spent two years in trekking work for the League.

Divine Enterprise

With the death of Reader Harris, in 1909, the League lost a highly respected leader, respected both within the League and far beyond. The leadership of the League of Prayer remained in the Harris family with Mary heading the work in the first instance, then their daughter and her husband, Howard Hooker, eventually taking over. Later the Rev Kenneth Howard Hooker who married the granddaughter of Reader Harris, and had served on the council as well as being Vice President to Mrs Howard Hooker, and had had an active ministry among students in Cambridge prior to his appointment as Vicar of Christ Church, Cockfosters, North London, in 1958, also served as President of the League, thus maintaining the link with the Harris family. Some years later he was succeeded by another Anglican clergyman, the Rev Maurice Winterburn, from the West Midlands, whose gracious and steady leadership strengthened the League and its ministry during his years in office when it sometimes seemed that the League was in terminal decline. Amongst many memories of Maurice, many will recall the dignified way in which he conducted Sunday morning worship in the chapel at the Hayes Conference Centre, Swanwick, during the annual convention.

The whole gospel for the whole man had been the concern of Reader and Mary Harris from the commencement of the mission at Speke Hall and through the ministry of the League. John Wesley had declared: "the gospel of Christ knows no religion, but social; there is no holiness but a social holiness." The Harris's fully embraced this and dedicated themselves to the cause of God's poor. The need of the lost was a reality for them and overseas missions a priority. It was to this that they called their workers. But no service could be successful without the worker experiencing his personal Pentecost. Reader Harris had remained convinced that the way to reach the world was through sanctified church members.   The evangelisation of the world, he wrote, is a Divine enterprise and can only be successful by Divine methods and under Divine inspiration and power.   The expectation of the early pre-millennial return of Christ added urgency to the task.   The key was mission and essential for mission was holiness.   Harris and the League of Prayer shared this outlook with the Holiness movement.   To this task Harris called his followers, both men and women.

Signs of the Awakening

Stories of successful missions abound in the League's magazine, *Tongues of Fire*, but few, if any, could be regarded as revival, if by revival we mean a work so sudden that none could accuse it of being contrived, and so deep and lasting in its results that all have to acknowledge that only God could have achieved such a work.

Looking back, however, we can see signs of the coming Awakening.   We have already mentioned that in January 1903, David Thomas and Rees Thomas led a mission in Carmarthen at the invitation of the Free Church Council.   Reader Harris joined them for the last few days.   This is described in *Tongues of Fire* as being first a week of services for intercessory prayer, led by local ministers, yet the mission report was dubbed "A Welsh Revival" and continued: "The remarkable effect of unity in the prosecution of Christian work has had a vivid illustration in Carmarthen."   As a result a strong League Centre was formed in the town and the impact of the League was not lost on the community or its ministers some of whom were instrumental in the Awakening of 1904, usually called the Welsh Revival.   One of the ministers, the Rev W.W. Lewis, a popular Presbyterian, was baptised with the Holy Spirit as he yielded his whole life to Christ in a cottage meeting.   It was an experience that was to prepare him for his role during and after the Revival.   Another minister, a Congregationalist, the Rev Professor Keri Evans, was influenced by Henry Drummond and made an act of consecration to Christ.   It was at a convention arranged by Reader Harris and the Pentecostal League, when R.B. Jones made a call to holiness that, after a bitter struggle, Evans found the grace to say "Yes, Lord."   He later testified to being "baptised with floods of living, mighty, transforming power for about half an hour.   It made me feel clean, whole and radiant to the very depths of my being."   These ministers met with F.B. Meyer at

Llandrindod Wells (where an annual convention continues to this day) for a Keswick type convention, and during the 1904-5 Revival, in which Evan Roberts was a prominent figure, and after in the teaching conventions that followed, they were to have prominent roles. It seems clear therefore that the League of Prayer played a significant part in this revival, a revival that swept through Wales and beyond to other lands. From its earliest days in Battersea the influence of the League of Prayer was felt all over the world.

As the name suggests, at the heart of the League was prayer. It would be a serious omission if we failed to point out that the League existed to foster prayer among God's people. The League was active in other ministries but prayer was the heartbeat of it all. Among his many booklets, Reader Harris had one entitled *Thousands Praying* with a publication figure of forty thousand. Central to all his work was the conviction that the Wesleyan emphasis on a second work of grace resulting in personal sanctification and the campaign for social holiness ought to be the normal experience of every believer.

Significant Personalities

Over the years, as the League of Prayer pursued its ministry, its great strength lay in its local and regional centres. Led by dedicated district secretaries with the support of a committed membership, the influence of the League continued in many areas of the country. Centres as far apart as Sunderland and Cornwall drew strong support. From its earliest days, the League of Prayer has been a lay movement with some choice saints from every walk of life, who have testified to the sanctifying grace of God in their lives. There can be little doubt that their witness as salt and light was a wholesome and illuminating presence in a dark and corrupt world.

This may be an appropriate point to name a representative group from those who made an indispensable contribution to the League and helped to give the League its distinctive ethos. Many more faithfully kept alive the message entrusted by God to Reader Harris years before. Centres in the South West maintained a vigorous work up to very recent days. David Foot Nash, a solicitor from Plymouth and a past Vice President of the Methodist Conference, was the national chairman of the League for a number of years. Gladys, his wife, wrote *A Corn of Wheat*, thus adding to the body of holiness literature. Miss Edith Tappin was a great soul-

14

winner who saw thirty of her thirty-three staff at the Outlands Nursing Home won for the Lord.

Another Plymouth man, Jim Tong, ran a residential convention at Teignmouth, and Norman Pritchard was leader of a very active League centre at St Austell. Willie Rodda of the famous Cornish Cream firm was another influential figure. For many years, William Burton was leader of the Chacewater meeting, of which the Quenchwell Convention was a part. Miriam, his daughter, later succeeded him, supported by her sister, Ruth Pengelly. Mervin Symons was (and still is) leader of the League centre at Launceston and indeed meetings will continue to take place under his leadership. Some colourful characters have enriched the League over the years, including Roy Pearce, a farmer from Fowey, who regularly attended the annual Swanwick Convention and was a great prayer warrior. A big man, strong and silent, with a tanned, open face of one who spent his days out of doors, Roy's spirituality and uncompromising testimony was a blessing to all who knew him. Another notable member, loved by all who attended the Swanwick Convention, was from Middleton, Lancashire. Miss Edith Hudson reached her 100th birthday in April 2009. Jean Harrop of Oldham, another League member, attended a birthday celebration in the residential home where Edith lived. Edith, who is now with the Lord, attended her first convention when she was nineteen and her last in 2003. The League played an important part in her life for seventy years, and she owed it so much for spiritual blessings she received through its ministry down the years. Another of her great friends, along with Jean, was Joyce Gautrey, who was called Home to be with the Lord some months ago. Joyce delighted in saying that her first link with the League was on the day she was born. Her father fetched the nurse out of a League of Prayer meeting at Speke Hall! One evening in January 1941, in answer to her prayer, the Lord cleansed her heart and filled her with the Holy Spirit. In May of that year, she became a student at Emmanuel Bible College, Birkenhead, hoping to serve the Lord overseas, an ambition that unfortunately did not materialise, though she continued to 'walk the talk', fulfilling a gracious ministry to those who came within the orbit of her influence. She returned to the League in 1970 when she attended a monthly meeting in the home of Kenneth and Ruth Bolton, in Croydon, where she lived. Later Joyce became a valued member of the League Council. To mention Ken Bolton is to recall his brother, Charlie, who was the leader of a League group in Liverpool. George Wood, the godly leader of the League centre at Onwood Hall, Manchester, and a worthy member of the council for a number of years, was miraculously healed of the last stages of bowel cancer, and lived into his late eighties. Apparently, his healing produced a beautiful youthful complexion! From the North West and League centres in Manchester, Oldham, Bolton and elsewhere, we move across country to the North East to arrive at the strong League centre at Sunderland and the dedicated leadership of Alice Duckas who is active to this day. Her meeting still attracts a good attendance of believers eager to hear the message of full salvation. Jim Osman, of Shiney Row, was another significant figure in that area.

A number of able men served the League as General Secretary, among them the Rev E.J. (Jack) Maddock, in the 1930s, who came to the League from the Spezia Mission, Italy, and was followed by the Rev J.H. Stringer. After succeeding John Sutherland Logan, a former Salvation Army officer, who had been appointed as President of Vennard College, USA, the Rev Percy Hassam, of whom mention has already been made, served as General Secretary, and travelled the length and breadth of England taking services and promoting the League, after its downturn during the Second World War. The Revs Gordon Brayshaw and Douglas A. Crossman served as Travelling Secretary for a brief period, the latter also editing its magazine.

Centenary Celebrations

Many noted holiness leaders have lent their support as speakers at conventions, particularly the Annual Convention at Swanwick. These included the Rev Duncan Campbell of the Faith Mission, known the world over as a leader in the revival on the Isle of Lewis (1949-1952), the Revs Sydney Martin, Stanley Banks, Maynard James, Major Allister Smith, the Rev Drs Denis Applebee, Herbert McGonigle, Peter W. Gentry, Alec Passmore, Arthur Skevington Wood, Colin Peckham and Rev Leslie Evans who, for many years served as General Director and Secretary of the League, to name but a few. Leslie Evans' writings are featured in Part Two of this book. There were many others – preachers and soloists - whom space will not allow to be listed but whose ministry has enriched and challenged the lives of countless believers over the years.

In the year 1991, the League celebrated its centenary with special gatherings up and down the country; at Plymouth, Birmingham, Rotherham, Clapham Junction and Sunderland. The General Director, to commemorate the start of the work at that venue, dedicated a Remembrance Table at Clapham Junction. The Swanwick Convention that year included a banquet meal with greetings from Michael Reader Harris and Dame Diana Reader Harris and a centenary cake presented by the Harris family. The Rev Leslie Evans and Dr Colin Peckham were the speakers, with Ian Awdas as soloist. To mark the centenary, Albert Harper's book, *The Real Thing*, was reissued with the title, *Life in the Spirit*.

Over the years, the League has maintained close relationships with other holiness movements, including the Faith Mission, Japan Evangelistic Band, the Irish Evangelistic Band, and the Grace Wesleyan Trust. The Rev Frank Webster founded the latter group in Cardiff. Following his sudden death, Diane Robinson led a group of committed supporters who continued the work, tirelessly spending themselves in convention and Bible study work. Sadly after a long illness when she was selflessly cared for by her friend, Nova Gill, she answered her Home Call in September 2008. Diane was a valued member of the League of Prayer Council. More recently the League has developed strong links with the Wesley Fellowship. The League of Prayer would have been seriously impoverished had it not been for the efficient administrative skills of Alistair and Valerie Barclay. In Valerie the League had an irreplaceable secretary whose sudden Home Call in October 2009 dealt a severe blow to an increasingly fragile movement.

To adapt Hebrews 11, "And what more shall I say? For the time would fail me to tell of ..." Stanley F. and Bettine Ward, Reg Gates, Margaret and Fred Anderson, Sam Doherty, Kath and Derek Dolling, Harry and Shirley Harbage, Ken Moulds, Rosemary Hooker, and many more, including Trevor Roberts whose spiritual gift, he said, was 'helps'. Though small of stature, at the Swanwick Convention, he insisted on carrying luggage for the delegates, and was a self-appointed steward at the meetings. All have obtained a good testimony through faith, and many have now met the Lord face to face.

Shadow of Reader Harris

This small book recognises and celebrates the work of the League of Prayer over the past one hundred and twenty years, since its founding in Battersea in 1891. It includes a brief and inadequate sketch of a movement which has been described as "one of the best kept secrets in the Christian scene in the UK". The question presents itself as to what would have happened among the churches in Britain had they embraced the message and vision of Reader Harris and had it been realised in the lives of Christian believers throughout the land. The shadow of Reader and Mary Harris falls on our generation today with the urgent call to all concerned believers to continue to make their threefold focus a priority. God alone knows the timing of the coming revival. In His time He will pour out His blessing. Meanwhile our task is to, first of all, examine our own hearts, and then consecrate our lives afresh to His service, especially the demanding work of intercessory prayer for the revival of the churches and holy living in the fullness and enabling power of the Holy Spirit.

Oh! Breath of life, come sweeping through us,

Revive Thy Church with life and power;

Oh! Breath of life, come, cleanse, renew us,

And fit Thy Church to meet this hour.

Elizabeth A.P. Head (1850-1936).

PART TWO

Devotional Readings

THE GOD OF BEGINNINGS

Behold, I will do a new thing, now it shall spring forth; shall you not know it? I will even make a road in the wilderness (Isaiah 43: 19).

This is the word we need to hear and a promise we need to claim. Isaiah often finds encouragement in recalling the past. "Remember the former things of old, for I am God, and there is no other; I am God, and there is none like Me" (46: 9). The people were asked not only to remember the things of old, but also to walk in the old ways. " ... Ask for the old paths, where the good way is, and walk in it" (Jeremiah 6: 16). This is a salutary reminder that novelty for its own sake can never achieve the deep purposes of God or bring blessing to us. Our lives and our service must be built upon the unchanging nature of God and His unchanging purposes for His church, the world and us.

So with one hand we hold on to the tried and tested ways of God, but with the other we grasp hold of the new things He is seeking to do for us and through us. In one of his essays, F.W. Boreham writes: "God is an inveterate beginner! He is for ever and ever beginning, and, when the things He begins lose the energy with which He began them, He begins all over again."

God's 'new things' come because God's people bring a new faith to His promises, a new vision to their task, a new commitment to the ministry of prayer, a new openness to the Holy Spirit, a new confidence in the message of the gospel. We are called to pray for revival, but what is revival if it is not God doing some new thing in the world? As God's people let us seek afresh the life-giving rivers promised by Jesus in the gift of the Holy Spirit. – LE

A prayer:
Lord Jesus, help me to walk in the old ways, but give me the faith to expect the 'new things' you have promised to your people. Amen.

A HIGHWAY FOR GOD

Prepare the way of the Lord; make straight in the desert a highway for our God (Isaiah 40: 3).

"Prepare the way of the Lord, make straight paths for Him." These words, written originally in Isaiah 40: 3, are repeated by Matthew, Mark and Luke, seeing their fulfilment in the ministry of John the Baptist. There is no doubt that the people who first heard them would understand the real life situation which lay behind this verse. The roads in the East were notoriously bad, often just dirt tracks. Travel was hazardous, often dangerous, and almost always extremely uncomfortable. In fact there was a proverb in biblical times which said: "There are three states of misery – sickness, hunger and travel."

Some of the richer kings and rulers would have the roads roughly surfaced. These were known as the King's Highway. When a king planned to travel he would send a messenger ahead to instruct the people to prepare the road for him. When the Queen travels abroad (and at home) officials go to the various countries to plan and prepare for the visit. They ensure that no detail is overlooked – travel arrangements, accommodation, food, protocol – they prepare the way for the sovereign.

In a spiritual sense, John the Baptist prepared the road ahead for Jesus, making ready for the King. But he also called the people to prepare the way.

The voice of one crying in the wilderness: Prepare the way of the Lord; make His paths straight. Every valley shall be filled and every mountain and hill brought low; the crooked places shall be made straight and the rough ways smooth; and all flesh shall see the salvation of God (Luke 3: 4-6).

We can never manufacture revival, it must come from the Lord. But we must prepare the way for Him. Early Christians were called The Way. Is my life a way? A way of prayer, of holiness, of faith, of obedience? We need to be sure that we do not hinder but smooth the way of the Lord. – LE

A prayer:
Lord, help me to be, not an obstruction to you, but a way. Amen.

THE CENTRAL GOAL
We make it our aim … to be well pleasing to Him (2 Corinthians 5: 9).

"We make it our aim …" It requires a conscious decision and effort to keep our primary goal constantly in front of us. It means holding ourselves to the highest priority year in and year out; not making our first priority to win souls, or to establish churches, or to have revivals, but seeking only to be well pleasing to Him. It is not a lack of spiritual experience that leads to failure, but a lack of working to keep our eyes focused and on the right goal. At least once a week examine yourself before God to see if your life is measuring up to the standard He has for you. Paul was like a musician who gives no thought to audience approval if he can only catch a look of approval from his Conductor.

Any goal we have that diverts us even to the slightest degree from the central goal of being "approved to God" (2 Timothy 2: 15) may result in our rejection from service for Him. When you discern where the goal leads, you will understand why it is so necessary to keep "looking unto Jesus" (Hebrews 12: 2). Paul spoke of the importance of controlling his own body so that it would not take him in the wrong direction. He said: "I discipline my body and bring it into subjection, lest … I myself should be disqualified" (1 Corinthians 9: 27).

I must learn to relate everything to the primary goal, maintaining it without interruption. My worth to God publicly is measured by what I really am in my private life. Is my primary goal in life to please Him and to be acceptable to Him, or is it something less, no matter how lofty it may sound? – LE

A prayer:

All to Jesus I surrender,
Lord, I give myself to Thee;
Fill me with Thy love and power,
Let Thy blessing rest on me.

Judson W. Van de Venter (1855 – 1939)

THE DAILY RENEWED VOW

I beseech you therefore, brethren, by the mercies of God, that you present your bodies a living sacrifice, holy, acceptable to God, which is your reasonable service" (Romans 12: 1).

In order to obtain the blessing of a clean heart, God demands of us an entire consecration of our life to Himself. If we have made that consecration, and if our consecration is real, it meant that there and then we consecrated all that we had and were, and all that we ever hoped to be and have. We presented to Him our present capabilities, and implicit in that presentation was the promise that any further capabilities, which we may acquire as we matured in life and experience would likewise be dedicated to Him. The working out of the holiness of God in our daily life means that we *daily* honour that vow.

What does that mean? It means a constant adjustment of our life. We vowed to the Lord that we were willing for every sin to go, and for every idol to be broken down. God takes us at our word and as we walk in His light He unfolds one by one things that need to be adjusted, the habits that need to be broken off, and the indulgences that need to be abandoned. He asks us, as we face each particular thing: "Are you willing to let My holiness work out in your life in this respect?" "Will you let your body be a fit place for the Holy Ghost to indwell?"

It means perfect love in our heart. We told the Lord that we would love Him with all our heart, and that we would love our neighbour as ourselves. … Working out the salvation that God has wrought in means that in every experience of daily living we learn to manifest His love.

It means a willing readiness to obey. We also told the Lord that we would go where He wanted us to go and do what He wanted us to do. If we are to develop a holy character and manifest holy conduct, there will have to be a perpetual carrying out of our vows of consecration, a working out of what God has worked in us. – RH

A prayer:
O Jesus, I have promised to serve Thee to the end. Give me grace to follow, my Master and my Friend. - John Ernest Bode (1816 – 74)

MORE THAN FORGIVENESS

For sin shall not have dominion over you, for you are not under law but under grace (Romans 6: 14).

Dr W.E. Sangster wrote: "God can do more with our sin than forgive it." He was reminding the church that the Christian message is a message of forgiveness – but it was more! Of course, forgiveness is the basic need we all have in our dealings with God. None of us can come to God clean. The first prayer we all need to pray is: "God be merciful to me, a sinner." In the words of Dr H.R. Mackintosh: "Pardon is not the end of God's ways with men, but it is the blessing which leads in all others by the hand."

But is forgiveness, wonderful and necessary as it is, the best that we can expect from God? Paul strikes a gospel note we all need to hear when he wrote: "Sin shall not have dominion over you." Does that text mock us? Do we say to ourselves: "It is just not true! I find myself beaten again and again! Sin does have mastery over me." On the authority of God's Word we need to be reminded that we can win. There is an idea abroad, held by many Christian people, that sin is inevitable in the Christian's life, and that talk of victory over sin is unrealistic and unattainable.

We are not concerned about scoring doctrinal points, but we must be concerned about what God's Word says on this important matter. Is it possible for a Christian to live in victory over sin – can we win? In Romans chapter 6, Paul is dealing with the problem posed by the argument that God's grace can be used as an excuse for sinning. But Paul is pointing in exactly the opposite direction. Grace abounds so that we can know victory over sin. We are destined to win; it is for this reason that grace is given.

It is plenteous grace! Abounding! Springing up! Holiness of heart and life is possible because "where sin abounded grace did much more abound." Grace is always greater than the power of sin; there is victory in Jesus. Hallelujah! – LE

A prayer:

Plenteous grace in Thee is found,
Grace to cover all my sin;
Let the healing streams abound,
Make and keep me pure within.

Charles Wesley (1707 – 88)

REVIVAL – THE NEED FOR VISION

Who may ascend into the hill of the Lord? Or who may stand in His holy place?
He who has clean hands and a pure heart ..." (Psalm 24: 3,4).

It has been said that "revival is not normally something which comes upon the church of God unless people somewhere are moving with the vision of it." That is surely true. And therefore there must be an urgent need to ask God to give a fresh vision for revival. More than praying for revival, we must have a new vision, a new longing, a new expectation of the Lord's working created in our hearts.

Small prayer groups can be encouraged with the fact that revival has often commenced in the past through such groups. Colin Whitaker, in *Great Revivals,* tells how the Hebrides Revival of 1949 began:

Peggy Smith was eighty-four years old and blind. Her sister Christine, two years younger, was almost doubled up with arthritis. Yet in the early hours of a winter's morning in 1949, in a little cottage near Barnas village, on the Isle of Lewis in the Scottish Hebrides, they were to be found in earnest prayer. That morning God visited them in a special way, giving them an unshakable assurance that the revival they and others had been praying about for months, was near. Peggy told her sister: "This is what God promised, 'I will pour water upon him that is thirsty, and floods upon dry ground,' and we are dealing with a covenant-keeping God."

At the same time, God came to a group praying in a barn not far away, seeking God for revival. During the time of prayer a young man stood up and read from Psalm 24. After reading the passage a second time, he said: "Brethren, we have been praying for weeks. But I would like to ask: 'Are our hands clean? Is our heart pure?'" With that God's awesome presence swept the barn and, at four in the morning, in the words of Duncan Campbell, "they moved out of the realm of the common and the natural into the sphere of the supernatural. And that is revival."

It is this sense of God's presence we need today. – LE

A prayer:
Lord, cleanse my hands and cleanse my heart. Move and quicken your church to bring glory and honour to your name and to meet the challenge of today. Amen.

A SLAVE OR A KING

To Him who loved us and washed us from our sins in His own blood, and has made us kings and priests to His God and Father, to Him be glory and dominion forever and ever. Amen (Revelation 1: 5, 6).

Man was originally created to reign and was invested with kingly dignity. God said to him: "Have dominion over ... every living thing that moves on the earth" (Genesis 1: 28). And while Adam was obedient to God he did so reign. The earth brought forth of herself that which he required, the creatures were his willing subjects, and Adam was God's viceroy. But when Adam fell by yielding to another lord, the kingly power departed from him, the earth yielded thistles, and the creatures were no longer subject to him.

All was changed. Satan supplanted God in Adam, and supplied Adam and his descendants with counterfeits of kingly dignity and kingly power. Satan had said to Eve: "Ye shall be as gods" (Genesis 3: 5, *AV*), that is to say, independent. Man can never be independent. There is only one independent Being, and that is God Himself. Man must always be dependent. Eve believed the devil, and Adam and Eve became not as gods, as the devil had promised, but as slaves [and] has striven to shut God Almighty out of his heart and frustrate God's redemptive grace.

All through this time God has maintained His claim upon man; indeed the history of the world has just been the history of this strange controversy – man insisting upon being the devil's slave, and God offering to man not only liberty from slavery but a spiritual restoration to the kingly power, to the kingly dignity, and to the kingly occupation. God promised to bruise Satan's head, that is to say, to destroy his authority; and through the Old Testament period for thousands of years, the faithful men of God believed in the *coming* Christ, and wonderful saints some of them were. RH

A prayer:
Faithful and unchanging God, we are humbled as we remember that while we were yet sinners, in love your Son our Saviour died on the Cross for us. Help us by your grace to live our lives to your praise and glory. Amen.

ONE SPIRIT, ONE BODY

As the body is one and has many members, but all the members of that one body, being many, are one body, so also is Christ (1 Corinthians 12: 12).

When Jesus was on earth with a human body, He moved and acted through the instrumentality of His personal body. But the Christ in glory today moves and acts and lives out His life through His Body the Church. By the word church, I do not mean the Church of England, or the Wesleyan Church, or the Congregational Church, or the Baptist Church, or the Presbyterian Church, but I mean those men and women who through the dispensation have, as the word means, come out from idols to serve the living God and have been baptized with the Holy Spirit.

Christ's Body is not completed yet, and so His Kingdom is yet within us. When the Body is completed His Kingdom will be revealed about us, and He will bruise Satan's head with the foot of His Body. Every man and every woman in this dispensation is called by God to claim the mighty baptism of the Holy Ghost, so that they may be baptized by one Spirit into this one Body and have this great privilege and glorious honour. – RH

A prayer:
O God, our Father, your Church is made one by the indwelling of your Spirit. Grant that we as members of one Body may reveal your glory among all people and so bring honour to your holy name, through Jesus Christ our Lord. Amen.

DELIVERANCE FROM SIN

Therefore do not let sin reign in your mortal body, that you should obey it in its lusts (Romans 6: 12).

Throughout Christendom, from thousands of burdened hearts there comes the enquiry: to what extent can men and women be saved in this life? To answer such a question we must consult the Scriptures and examine the recorded testimonies of men. If the Bible does not promise deliverance from all sin, and if believers have experienced no such deliverance, it were futile to seek such deliverance. If on the other hand the Scriptures plainly teach, and the lips and pens of believers clearly affirm the truth of the experience, then every earnest soul may seek and find the blessing craved.

Definite clear scriptural teaching on the subject of deliverance from sin is of the utmost importance. Thousands upon thousands have practically been denied the experience of purity of heart by the uncertain teachings of their guides and instructors. Great and terrible indeed is the responsibility of those whose vague and uncertain, and sometimes grossly unscriptural teaching, has been used by the evil one to cloud the doctrine and spoil the experience of the fullness of the blessing of the gospel of Christ.

With infinite precision and divine definiteness the Holy Spirit has set forth in the Scriptures the full truth of abundant salvation. Our duty is plain: to examine the truth, to find out its plain meaning, and then to accept thankfully, faithfully, and thoroughly, what the Holy Spirit shows to be our right, privilege, and duty.

Our text is one of the great passages upon which faithful exponents of holiness have based their teaching. What is the plain meaning? "Our old man is [*RV* was] crucified with Him." This expression "our old man" is synonymous with "the flesh" in the Pauline use of the word. "They that are of Christ have crucified the flesh with the passions and the lusts thereof" (Galatians 5: 24, *RV*). Our whole sinful nature, which holds human nature in its thraldom, was crucified with Christ. – RH

A prayer:
O wretched man that I am! Who will deliver me from this body of death? I thank God, through Jesus Christ our Lord. Amen.

THE GREAT INTERCESSOR

I in them, and You in Me; that they may be made perfect in one, and that the world may know that You have sent Me, and have loved them as You have loved Me (John 17: 23).

Jesus when on earth contended against the kingdom of Satan by continual prayer and testimony. Pray with Him. He is the same Christ today. Who did He pray for? He prayed for His people. Read John 17. It is one of the great key chapters of the Bible. He prays for Himself, then He prays for the disciples who were about Him, and then He prays for somebody else: He prays for those "who shall believe" on Him "through their word." In other words, He prays for you, and for me, because every one of us believers is a believer through the word of His then disciples. He prays for us. What does He pray for us? He prays in the language of the verse at the head of this page.

That was His prayer on earth. He is the same Jesus Christ today, with the same heart of compassion, with the same yearning for His people, with the same longing for His Church, and with the same desires. He prays the same prayer today, I believe, for we are told in the Epistle to the Hebrews, that "He ever liveth to make intercession for us" (7: 25, *AV*). He is praying that prayer: "I in them, and thou, Father, in me, that they may be made perfect in one." Why? "That the world may get to know" – first, "that thou hast sent Me", and secondly, "that thou lovest them as thou lovest me."

That is your business, believer, and that is mine: to get the world around us to know through our testimony, and through our lives, that Jesus Christ was sent of God, and that God loves these poor, perishing sinners even as He loves Jesus Christ. Jesus prayed that prayer before the crucifixion; Jesus Christ the glorified prays that prayer today. Let us claim the needed grace that from our hearts and lips and lives and homes there shall go out the testimony that Jesus Christ was sent of God, and that God loves the world as He loves Jesus Christ. – RH

A prayer:
So, Lord, grant us that needed grace that, despite the devil's attacks, our consistent testimony – by word and deed – may demonstrate your love for all. Amen.

TWO MYSTERIES

And without controversy great is the mystery of godliness: God was manifested in the flesh, justified in the Spirit, seen by angels, preached among the Gentiles, believed on in the world, received up in glory (1 Timothy 3: 16).

Today we are face to face with two great mysteries. There is first, the 'mystery of iniquity', and by that I mean a world redeemed by the divine Love and divine Blood, a world that scorns the Redeemer is yet unconsumed. The second mystery is the 'mystery of God', the hidden Kingdom, the Kingdom within us. Christ tarries. Why? He is waiting for the completion of His Body. He is waiting for the cooperation of His people. God could sweep all evil out of this world with one single motion of His will, but He does not do so.

He is waiting for the cooperation of His people. But they must be holy, they must be pure, they must be baptized by one Spirit into one Body, so that they may be wholly and entirely ready for the divine will to be carried out through them. In a word, quick to learn the divine will and quick to obey it.

What then is our duty? The duty of every soul is first to ask itself: am I born again? Nine-tenths of the difficulties about holiness are traceable to the lack of definite, pungent, glorious experience of the new birth. Our Lord said: "Ye must be born again .... Except a man be born again he cannot see the Kingdom of God" (John 3: 3, 7).

If you are born again, then your duty is to seek this baptism "by one Spirit into one Body". Claim and occupy your place in the Body of Christ. That is the true place of the saint. Be swift to obey your Head. Receive largely of the Spirit, witness for Jesus Christ, do your part as far as in you lies to complete the Body of Christ, establish the Kingdom, move on with God. Above all, pray. - RH

A prayer:
Lord Jesus Christ, I would claim and occupy my place among your people and know the power of the risen Lord, even though it will involve sharing in your suffering, that I may do my part to complete your Body and establish your Kingdom. Amen.

AT THE WALL OF THE WORLD

If we walk in the light as He is in the light, we have fellowship with one another, and the blood of Jesus Christ His Son cleanses us from all sin (1 John 1: 7).

When Jesus Christ shed His blood on the Cross it was not the blood of a martyr, or the blood of one man for another, it was the life of God poured out to redeem the world. ... Our Lord did not sacrifice Himself for a cause; he poured out His life for a purpose in the mind of God. We will sacrifice ourselves to further orders for another part of ourselves, but the meaning of Jesus Christ's passion is that of the very heart of God, and when my eyes are open I see that Jesus Christ had made the basis of life redemptive, and it cost Him everything to do it. The death of Christ was not the death of a martyr, it was God manifesting Himself in the heart of the human race when the human race was saying, 'Crucify Him.'

The Christian revelation is not that Jesus Christ stands to us as the representative of God, but that He *is* God. If He is not, then we have no God. "... *God was in Christ* reconciling the world unto Himself" (2 Corinthians 5: 19). We do not worship an austere, remote God; He is here in the thick of it. The Cross is a reality, not a symbol: at the wall of the world stands God with His arms outstretched. There is nothing more certain in time or eternity than what Jesus Christ did on the Cross: He switched the whole human race back into right relationship to God and made the basis of human life redemptive, consequently any member of the human race can get in touch with God *now*. It means not simply that men are saved from Hell and put right for Heaven, but that they are freed from the wrong disposition and can have imparted to them the very disposition of the Son of God, viz., the Holy Spirit. – OC

A prayer:

May the mind of Christ my Saviour
Live in me from day to day,
By His love and power controlling
All I do and say.

Kate B. Wilkinson (1859 – 1928)

HOISTING OUR SAILS

Hezekiah and all the people rejoiced that God had prepared the people, since the events took place so suddenly (2 Chronicles 29: 36).

"The events took place so suddenly." These words are used to describe a remarkable Old Testament revival, which saw the cleansing of the Temple, the reinstitution of pure worship, and a new sense of God's presence and power in the nation. Moffatt's translation renders this same word: "For the thing had come as a sudden surprise!"

Sometimes the complaint is made that God seems to work very slowly. There is a proverb which gives support to this view: "The mills of God grind slowly, but they grind exceeding small." But there are also times when God works suddenly and surprises us by His swiftness. "The Lord, whom you seek, will *suddenly* come to His temple" (Malachi 3: 1). "When the Day of Pentecost had fully come, they were all with one accord in one place. And *suddenly* there came a sound from heaven, as of a rushing mighty wind" (Acts 2: 1, 2). And so Pentecost came as a swift, powerful and sudden new work of God.

But we need to face another truth in this chapter. While it is true that God worked quite suddenly, it is also true that this work was not independent of the people of God. Hezekiah rejoiced that God had prepared the people (verse 36). Dr Campbell Morgan commented: "We cannot manufacture revival, but we can hoist our sails to catch the winds of the Spirit when they blow." We must take this challenge to heart. Revival came suddenly but it was not isolated from the spiritual condition and response of the people. There was a definite preparation for this suddenness; there always has been and always will be.

In Hezekiah's day, Judah was being attacked from every side and the young king could have done what so many of us prefer today – blame everything and everyone else for the troubles that afflict us. But Hezekiah had the wisdom to start on the inside, for he forced the nation to face its own sin and need. Is it not true that if only we would allow God to prepare us we would see what we are praying for – a real move of the Spirit of God in our land again. – LE

A prayer:
Surely I am coming quickly. Amen. Even so, come, Lord Jesus!

34

THE WINDOWS OF OUR HEART

You are the salt of the earth ... You are the light of the world (Matthew 5: 13, 14).

God's order always is, "Beginning at Jerusalem." "Ye are the salt of the earth," He says, but if the salt has lost its savour what good is it? May God re-salt us, and keep this dark world from putrefaction. "Ye are the light of the world." Do we believe it? If we are to be the light of the world, we must be *above* the world. In too many cases the light of God in our hearts is not seen because it is under some worldly bushel. Let us break every pitcher that hinders the light from shining through us upon the dark world around us!!

Pentecost *is* repeatable. The need is admitted. Fulfil the conditions and you will receive the same blessing, and demonstrate the same results. I believe that every individual soul should have a Pentecost. God has poured out the Holy Ghost upon all flesh. He is here. We have not to cry to God to open the windows of heaven, He has done it. The need today is that we should open the windows of our hearts and let this heavenly Holy Ghost, in all His wondrous power, into every department of our being.

What are the conditions? They are the same as on the first day of Pentecost, when the early disciples, unknown, ignorant, working men and working women, tarried at Jerusalem and were filled with the Holy Ghost. The first thing to notice is that they were all on their knees. Fancy the whole church praying! That is the aim of the Pentecostal League of Prayer: that every believer shall learn to pray in the Holy Ghost. Prayer, like everything else, has to be taught. Prayer is not gabbling, or parroting! Prayer is talking to God, asking God in the name of Jesus Christ for what God has put in our hearts to desire. And prayer is not only asking but *receiving*. They were all on their knees. – RH

A prayer:
Lord God, show us that we would be steadier on our feet in witness and service for spending time regularly on our knees in earnest, believing prayer. Convict us of our need to make prayer the number one priority in our personal lives and in our church life, before all else. Lord, teach us to pray. Amen.

REDEEMED!

You were not redeemed with corruptible things, like silver or gold, from your aimless conduct received by tradition from your fathers, but with the precious blood of Christ, as of a lamb without blemish and without spot (1 Peter 1: 18, 19).

To be redeemed means we are not our own, we are bought with a price, as Paul says. Even our belief is not our own for it is by Christ that we believe in God (verse 21). Let us bring some practical questions to the subject.

From what are we redeemed? "From your vain manner of life handed down from your fathers" (verse 18, *RV*). The word 'vain' means empty, futile, non-productive and ineffective. And it is a hang-over from past generations. "It's in the blood," we say. We humans have come a very long way and parental blood streams of remote ancestry flow through our veins. Heredity plays a great part in human life. The Bible has a good deal to say about 'the fathers'. In Israel there was a proverb which said: "The fathers have eaten sour grapes and set the children's teeth on edge" (Ezekiel 18: 2, *RV*), by which proverb they meant, "We cannot help being what we are, we cannot help living in sin. Our fathers committed these sins and we are their children, therefore we are not responsible for our sins."

God has a great answer to this: "Behold, all souls are mine" (Ezekiel 18: 4, *RV*). We may bear physical resemblances to our fathers and they may even hand on their temperaments, but God says, "All souls are mine," and the end of our faith is the salvation of the soul.

This living soul that I call mine
Can think, and feel, and love.
It is an utterance of Thine,
A breathing from above.

There are three meanings of the word *redeemed:* (1) To deliver by payment; (2) To purchase out of the market, as a slave could be bought and then given his freedom; (3) To liberate – set free. All this and more is included in this wonderful redemption, God's remedy for sin. – PH

A prayer:
Holy Spirit, flow through my soul, redeem its desert places, and make a garden there for the Lord I adore. - Albert Orsborn.

WHY WERE WE REDEEMED?

As He who called you is holy, you also be holy in all your conduct (1 Peter 1: 15).

The answer is a life of holiness. "As he which called you is holy, be ye yourselves also holy in all manner of living" (1: 15). Said a convert: "The Cross of Jesus condemns me to be a saint!" When I survey the wondrous Cross can I contemplate any other kind of life than a holy life? But this life of holiness is not by effort of my own, it is the gift of the Holy Spirit, "in sanctification of the Spirit" (verse 2). It is the gift of God imparted by the Spirit. He has bought us to possess us. "Being made free from sin and become servants of God, ye have your fruit unto sanctification, and the end is eternal life" (Romans 6: 22, *RV*). This life will have a great outreach: "Then the nations shall know that I am the Lord, saith the Lord God, when I shall be sanctified in you before their eyes" (Ezekiel 36: 23, *RV*). The testimony of a holy life is irrefutable and far-reaching in its witness.

Finally, we are redeemed into the inheritance of the sanctified. Look at verses 3 – 5. "Blessed be the God and Father of our Lord Jesus Christ, who according to His great mercy begat us again into a living hope by the resurrection of Jesus Christ from the dead, unto *an inheritance*, incorruptible and undefiled and that fadeth not away, reserved in heaven for you." What an inheritance this is! It is beyond death for it is *incorruptible*. It is beyond the power of sin for it is *undefiled*. It is beyond the forces of decay for it *fadeth not away.*

It is *reserved* not for the next life but for this life. It is for you who are kept by the power of God through faith unto a salvation yet to be revealed in the last time (verse 5). This is a reference to our final salvation, the redemption of the body – salvation from the presence of sin.

Verse 18 says, *"knowing this"*. Do we know it? God wants us to *know*. – PH

A prayer:

> *Answer that gracious end in me*
> *For which Thy precious life was given,*
> *Redeem from all iniquity,*
> *Restore and make me meet for Heaven.*
> *Unless Thou purge my every stain,*
> *Thy sufferings and my faith are vain.*
>
> Charles Wesley (1707 – 88)

THE PURCHASE OF BLOOD

Redeemed ... with the precious blood of Christ (1 Peter 1: 18, 19).

By what were we redeemed? Negatively, "not with silver or gold" (verse 18). There is an impotence about money in the spiritual realm. It has great power in the world, buying prestige and position, and multitudes worship the golden calf, but it all ends at the grave. Jesus said: "It is easier for a camel to go through the needle's eye than for a rich man to enter into the Kingdom of God (Matthew 19: 24, *RV*). Even in this life there are many things that cannot be bought with money. The balm of a guilty conscience, the restoration of broken vows, the cure for a lack of love. None of these respond to the call of money. Alone all silver and gold cannot redeem the soul; they may bring a doubtful refinement, but not redemption. Peter said to a man with wealth and influence: "Thy money perish with thee" (Acts 8: 20, *RV*).

Positively, we were redeemed with the precious blood of Christ. We are justified and we are sanctified through the blood of Christ (Hebrews 13: 12). If we have victory it is through the blood (Revelation 12: 11). Without the shedding of blood there is nothing in any realm that is worthwhile. The word 'to bleed' and 'to bless' come from the same Anglo Saxon root. Only the bleeding heart can bless. How much more is this wonderful redemption?

> *Oh, make me understand it,*
> *Help me to take it in,*
> *What it meant to Thee, the Holy One,*
> *To bear away my sin.*
>
> Katherine A.M. Kelly (1869 – 1942)

Here is our worth to God. It is a "perfect redemption, the purchase of blood", and in the light of what has been said regarding the manner of life handed down from the fathers, how wonderful is the promise spoken by the prophet: "I will cleanse their blood that I have not cleansed" (Joel 3: 21, *RV*). Our redeeming God is greater than any family record. He breaks the entail. The Lamb takes all our sin away. – PH

A prayer:

> *Take all my sin away,*
> *O spotless Lamb, I come to Thee,*
> *Take all my sin away.*
>
> Salvation Army Chorus

38

A STEADY INWARD FIRE

Stephen, full of grace and power (Acts 6: 8).

"You shall be my witnesses," the Lord promised His disciples before He left them to return to His Father. In the Acts of the Apostles we see that promise abundantly fulfilled in those early Christians. So what was it that turned those often weak and defeated men into bold and effective witnesses for Him?

There was power in the church

"Stay," Jesus said, "until you have been clothed with power from on high." The pouring of the Holy Spirit upon them was the prerequisite of effective witnessing. Through Pentecost He was not only going to empower them for service, but would fill them with Himself that they might become the people that He wanted them to be. To be filled with the Spirit involved purity of heart, cleansing from sin, being set free from self-seeking. Henceforth they would have one purpose of heart – to obey God, to walk in holiness before Him, and to live for His glory alone. Perhaps that looks like three purposes, but they cannot be separated, just as it is inconceivable that the filling of the Holy Spirit can be separated from heart purity, for He is the *Holy* Spirit and God has called us to holiness (1 Peter 1: 15).

Those disciples were changed people after Pentecost. A.W. Tozer wrote: "Those early disciples burned with a steady, inward fire." Even the High Priest and his family "took note that they had been with Jesus". The work of the Spirit is the same now as it was then; to glorify God and to transform us into His likeness and to set us on the road to being effective witnesses. How? By purifying our hearts and filling us with Himself (Acts 15: 9).

That godly Scottish preacher, Robert Murray McCheyene, who died at the early age of twenty-nine, said: "To bring us to perfect holiness was the very end for which Christ died." His prayer was: "Lord, make me as holy as a pardoned sinner can be made." – JG

A prayer:
Lord, that is my prayer also. Make me as holy as a forgiven sinner can be made. Amen.

39

THE ATMOSPHERE OF PRAYER

And they continued steadfastly in the apostles' doctrine and fellowship, in the breaking of bread, and in prayers (Acts 2: 42).

There was a radiance about those early Christians. Stephen, a man full of God's grace and power, when falsely accused was radiant for his Lord. Even his enemies saw his face "as the face of an angel" (Acts 6: 15). The apostles rejoiced that they were counted worthy to suffer shame for His name, and the apostle Paul constantly spoke of his joy in the Lord. Their radiance was not dependent on circumstances, but on the indwelling presence of the Holy Spirit, who alone can produce that radiance of soul that will attract others to the Saviour. What made the difference?

There was prayer in the fellowship

Prayer in the Upper Room resulted in three thousand being saved on the day of Pentecost, and people being added daily to the church. Because the church prayed continually, revival came to Samaria and the Ethiopian trusted Christ. The prayer meeting was the essential part of the church's life, and mighty things were wrought through prayer. Oh, what God could and would accomplish if we would make prayer a priority in our lives. When the disciples prayed they were filled afresh with the Holy Spirit, and likewise if our lives are to be daily fresh and vibrant, then we too must breathe the very atmosphere of prayer. Prayer will do at least as much for us as for those for whom we pray. God is looking for intercessors.

Paul tells us that we do not wrestle against flesh and blood, but against principalities and powers, against spiritual wickedness. There is a battle going on, for Satan does not give up souls easily. Jesus Christ won the victory at Calvary, but those in the grip of evil will be released only through the power of Christ's precious blood, as we claim the victory in His name. In these days when wickedness abounds around us, let us give ourselves to prayer as the Early Church did, pleading the promises of God till He sends revival. Maybe it needs to begin in us! – JG

A prayer:
Holy Ghost, revival comes from Thee, send a revival, start the work in me. Amen.

EFFECTIVE WITNESSES

And they went out and preached everywhere, the Lord working with them and confirming the word through the accompanying signs (Mark 16: 20).

There was proclamation to the world.

When there is power in the church and prayer in the fellowship, there will inevitably be proclamation of the gospel to the world. No wonder people came to Christ! The disciples were strengthened in their ministry and against all threats of their enemies proclaimed the Word of God with boldness. With such power and prayer there was conviction of sin, repentance and turning to Christ as the gospel was proclaimed – the great need of the church and the world today. Even persecution only served to widen this proclamation, for as the disciples were scattered abroad, they witnessed to the Saviour wherever they went.

There was a price to be paid.

To witness for Christ can mean suffering and death. Quoting again from A.W. Tozer: "The story of the earliest Christians is a story of faith under fire. These first disciples turned to Christ with the full understanding that they were espousing an unpopular cause that would cost them everything.

The apostle Paul yearned that he might know Christ "and the power of His resurrection and the fellowship of His sufferings." How often we desire to know Him and the power of His resurrection but would rather escape the fellowship of His sufferings. For Christians in many countries today there is no other way. It was said of Jorge Gonzales, who gave his life for Christ in Colombia in 1996: "The Cross of Jesus had been indelibly imprinted across his life." So it was with the early disciples. So it must be with us if we would be effective witnesses for Him. There is a price to be paid. – JG

A prayer:

May I die daily to sin, count all things but loss,
In paths of righteousness walk, proclaiming your Word.
Stir me to lay hold of You, till revival You send
And men in repentance turn to their Saviour and Lord.

DESTINED TO BE HOLY
"... it is written, 'Be holy, for I am holy'" (1 Peter 1: 16).

We must continually remind ourselves of the purpose of life. We are not destined to happiness, nor to health, but to holiness. Today we have far too many desires and interests, and our lives are being consumed and wasted by them. Many of them may be right, noble and good, and may later be fulfilled, but in the meantime God must cause their importance to us to decrease. The only thing that truly matters is whether a person will accept the God who will make him holy. At all costs, a person must have the right relationship with God.

Do I believe I need to be holy? Do I believe that God can come into me and make me holy? If through your preaching you convince me that I am unholy, I then resent your preaching. The preaching of the gospel awakens an intense resentment because it is designed to reveal my lack of holiness, but it also awakens an intense yearning and desire within me. God has only one intended destiny for mankind – holiness. His goal is to produce saints. God is not some eternal blessing machine for people to use, and He did not come to save us out of pity. Rather He came to save us because He created us to be holy. Atonement through the Cross of Christ means that God can put me back into perfect oneness with Himself through the death of Jesus Christ, without a trace of anything coming between us any longer.

Never tolerate because of sympathy for yourself or for others, any practice that is not in keeping with a holy God. Holiness means absolute purity of your walk before God, the words coming from your mouth, and every thought in your mind. This means placing every detail of your life under the scrutiny of God Himself. Holiness is not simply what God gives me, but what God has given me that is being exhibited in my life. – OC.

A prayer:
Purge me with hyssop, and I shall be clean; wash me, and I shall be whiter than snow .... Create in me a clean heart, O God, and renew a right spirit within me ... Restore to me the joy of Your salvation and uphold me by Your generous Spirit (Psalm 51).

GRACIOUS UNCERTAINTY
"... it has not yet been revealed what we shall be ..." (1 John 3: 2).

Our natural inclination is to be so precise, trying always to forecast accurately what will happen next, so much so that we look upon uncertainty as a bad thing. We think that we must reach some predetermined goal, but that is not the nature of the spiritual life. The nature of the spiritual life is that we are certain in our uncertainty. Consequently we do not put down roots. Our common sense asks: "What if I were in that circumstance?" We cannot presume to see ourselves in any circumstance in which we have never been.

Certainty is the mark of the common sense life; gracious uncertainty is the mark of the spiritual life. To be certain of God means that we are uncertain in all our ways, not knowing what tomorrow may bring. This is generally expressed with a sigh of sadness, but it should be an expression of breathless expectation. We are uncertain of the next step, but we are certain of God. As soon as we abandon ourselves to God and do the task He has placed closest to us, He begins to fill our lives with surprises. When we become simply a promoter or a defender of a particular belief something within us dies. That is not believing God, it is only believing our belief about Him. Jesus said: "... unless you ... become as little children ..." (Matthew 18: 3). The spiritual life is the life of a child. We are not uncertain of God, just uncertain of what He is going to do next. If our certainty is only in our beliefs, we develop a sense of self-righteousness, become overly critical, and are limited by the view that our beliefs are complete and settled. But when we have the right relationship with God, life is full of spontaneous, joyful uncertainty and expectancy. Jesus said: "... believe also in Me" (John 14: 1), not "believe certain things about Me." Leave everything to Him and it will be gloriously and graciously uncertain how He will come in, but you can be certain He will come in. Remain faithful to Him. – OC

A prayer:
Praise you, Lord, that we have received a Kingdom that cannot be shaken. Grant us grace that we may serve You acceptably with reverence and godly fear. Amen.

THE LAW OF THE CRUCIFIED LIFE

The law of the Spirit of life in Christ Jesus has made me free from the law of sin and death (Romans 8: 2).

The key to an understanding of the New Testament's words about 'death to sin' lies in its tense. "He that is dead is freed from sin" (Romans 6: 7). Not he that *was* dead five years or five minutes ago, but he that *is* dead, at this moment. Moment by moment we are kept in His love. Let me illustrate. Here are two Electricity Board linesmen working on a high-tension cable. "Is this line dead?" shouts the linesman aloft. He doesn't want to know from his mate whether the line *was* dead half an hour ago. He wants to know whether it *is* dead. He must know what the reaction will be if he touches the line now.

So with my state of deadness to sin. If, when the sudden temptation is presented to my mind, I remember that I am a sanctified Christian, that I am not my own, that this "mind" must be in me which was also in Christ Jesus, that I must "reckon" myself to be dead indeed to this sin and alive unto God (Romans 6: 11), that it is my business to see that my reaction to this temptation is the reaction that a pathologist gets from a corpse under post-mortem examination, then I at once face up to the fact that the old David Foot Nash, who would have fallen for this temptation, now hangs on the Cross, "in" Christ, and is, poor fellow (!) past all responding to the temptation's power.

It has taken me several minutes to write the foregoing sentences, but, when I am entirely sanctified, it means that I have made up my mind beforehand what my "reckoning", what my reaction, is going to be to sin; and then, in an instant, the indwelling Spirit of God can warn me, when the temptation comes, that *this is the moment* to operate the law of the crucified life. If, in obedience to His urgent whisper, I at once present to the temptation a reaction of deadness, if I am dead to sin, lo! I am "alive unto God", and "the law of the Spirit of life in Christ Jesus had made me free from the law of sin and death" (Romans 8: 2) – DFN

A prayer:
Lord, may I know such a sensibility of sin when temptation presents itself that I may catch the wandering of my will and quench the kindling fire. Amen.

A DROP IN A BUCKET

The kingdom of heaven is like a mustard seed, which a man took and sowed in his field, which indeed is the least of all seeds; but when it is grown it is greater than the herbs and becomes a tree, so that the birds of the air come and nest in its branches (Matthew 13: 31, 32).

More often than not, when faced with some of the great challenges of life, we feel so small and insignificant. It is the frustration we feel when we see television pictures of thousands of children starving to death in Africa and we wonder what we can do in the face of such overwhelming disaster. It is the same question which comes to disturb us as we think about the moral and spiritual needs of our nation.

The Christian enterprise seems so weak in the face of such challenges. Maybe it was to counter this mood that Jesus gave us the parable of the mustard seed. Our Lord is reminding us that the real test of the Kingdom of God is not size but vitality – the life-force of the seed.

Film Director Samuel Goldwyn once remarked that he wanted a film which began with an earthquake and worked up to a climax! With that aspiration he was stating a very human tendency: to worship the large and spectacular. But Jesus always saw the Kingdom, not as being statistically large, but dynamically alive.

The history of revival illustrates the truth that vitality is mightier than size. Many times it has been the handful who have kept on praying, in spite of all that seemed to be opposed to the gospel, who have seen God work in power and victory. Dr James Stewart observed: "We talk about the 'High Church', 'Low Church', 'Broad Church', but what Christ wants is the *Deep* Church." He adds that the Church is made up of those who have sunk their lives deep into Christ. – LE

A prayer:
Dear Lord, give us the faith to believe that our prayers make a difference and keep us faithful in continuing to seek Your face for revival. Amen.

PRAYING AND NOT FAINTING

[Jesus said], Men always ought to pray and not lose heart (Luke 18:1).

The Bible has a great deal to say about fainting! No child of God seems to be exempt from the peril of its possibility, for we read in Isaiah 40: 30: "Even the youths shall faint and be weary." In Deuteronomy 20: 8, there was a standing order that regulated all battles in which God's people took part, and this is how it reads: "The officers shall speak further to the people, and say, 'What man is there who is fearful and fainthearted? Let him go and return to his house, lest the heart of his brethren faint like his heart.'"

There is an awful contagion about faintheartedness. What is this insidious thing? Physically, fainting is a temporary blackout, a loss of consciousness. Spiritually, it is a collapse of the spirit, a loss of spiritual vitality. When that happens anything may follow. We may lose courage and the joy of the Lord, which is always our strength, give up the struggle and cease to work for God.

Jesus speaks with authority on this subject when He says: "Men ought always to pray, and not to faint." No man ever prayed as He did. No man ever taught the power of prayer more earnestly than our blessed Lord, and here He says that the one antidote to a fainting Christian life is always to pray. There are three ways of getting things done in this world: by *thinking*, by *working*, and by *praying*. A modern writer has said: "There are things that God cannot do unless men *pray*." Oh, that we would recapture the wonder of prayer! It surpasses the wonder of wireless, for by radio a man is linked up to men, but in prayer he is in communication with God.

If radio's slim fingers can pluck a melody
From night and toss it o'er a continent and sea;
If songs like crimson roses are called from thin blue air,
Why should mortals wonder if God hears prayer?

The radio brings together different parts of the Earth, but prayer brings Earth and Heaven together. – LE

A prayer:
Lord, teach us to pray. Amen.

IN CHRIST

That He might present her to Himself a glorious church, not having spot or wrinkle or any such thing, but that she should be holy and without blemish (Ephesians 5: 27).

Our Lord is God's truth incarnate, God's ideal in the flesh. God gave His final revelation in Christ and then set processes at work to make His ideal a reality in the lives of many more people in the character of Christians who are His truth incorporated in flesh and blood.

You see, in pursuits such as art, music and literature, the ideal is a great vague end toward which all artisans evolve their work more or less blindly. But in spiritual pursuits, we have the ideal manifested in flesh and blood, and we can measure certainly our growing up into Him in all things (Ephesians 4: 12, 13).

Being in Christ does not mean that somehow God pretends we are all right. It means that the Spirit of God in regeneration and the mighty baptism with the Holy Spirit recreates us. In this was that glorious Spirit-baptized community created, which is often called the Church.

I believe, however, that such a usage of the term 'church' is a misleading limitation of our Lord's meaning. When He refers to the church in Matthew 16: 18, for instance, we would be much nearer His meaning if we translated *ekklesia* as 'my new humanity', against which death and time have no power.

Being in Christ means proclaiming by my bodily life what is easily discerned to be the life of Jesus. It means that I am part of an innumerable host of the *ekklesia*, the new people in Christ (Ephesians 5: 25-27). - Anon

A prayer:
Lord Jesus, I am determined to live each day in your fullness. Amen.

THE HOPE OF OUR CALLING

In Him you also trusted, after you heard the word of truth, the gospel of your salvation, in whom also, having believed, you were sealed with the Holy Spirit of promise, who is the guarantee of our inheritance until the redemption of the purchased possession, to the praise of His glory (Ephesians 1: 13, 14).

As a young convert, one of the great evidences of the gospel of Jesus Christ was seen in the lives of ordinary men and women with whom I came into contact. The presence of the Lord radiated from their very faces, it was displayed in the way they talked, it dictated the way they lived, and above all, it shone through their spoken testimony. From a worldly standpoint, few of them had much of this world's goods. From a spiritual standpoint, however, they were rich beyond measure. It was the certainty of their faith that was so attractive. They did not hope, they believed! There is a big difference.

Is it true that we do not encounter the same certainty today? The hope of heaven remains. The belief that one day God will break into history again, and that hopefully there will be a place there for those who remain faithful. But my erstwhile friends didn't just hope for heaven, they believed they were going there! They sang about it with confidence: "When the roll is called up yonder, *I'll be there!*"

Paul gave the Christian Church at Ephesus a great note of encouragement in Ephesians 1: 13,14, quoted above. What a progression! You *heard* – the word of truth. You *trusted* – in Christ. You *believed* – in Christ. You were *sealed* - by Christ. Could it be that today we so often leave out step three? We hear the word of the gospel, we trust in and accept it for ourselves, and find salvation. We are sealed by that Spirit of promise that makes our adoption sure – *but do we believe it?*

The verses point to a second experience, which is the right of every believer through the work done for us on the Cross. When we are in no doubt about the riches of our inheritance in Christ we are then able to know the exceeding greatness of His power. It was not self-delusion that transformed the lives of those men and women of my youth; *it was belief!* – DD.

A prayer:
Lord, I do believe, but sometimes doubt almost overwhelms me. 'Help Thou my unbelief', I pray. Amen.

FLAT TYRE CHRISTIANITY
And they were all filled with the Holy Spirit (Acts 2: 4).

Not long before he died, in 1965, Karl Barth, the Swiss theologian, was asked what he thought of the religious situation in Britain and on the Continent. "What we are seeing," he replied, "is flat-tyre Christianity." The pneuma, which is Greek for both 'air' and 'spirit', has gone out of it, and everybody knows what happens to the pneumatic tyre when it loses its pneuma.

It was Pentecost which put the pneuma, the Spirit, into the Church of Christ and into the lives of the disciples. Modern advertising makes good use of the 'before and after' gimmick. For instance, it will show the human silhouette before and after using a certain diet product or exercise apparatus, and the difference is remarkable, some would say unbelievable!

If we apply the 'before and after' test to Pentecost there is no doubt that the result is very impressive indeed. Those disciples were very much like 'flat tyres' before Pentecost, but when the pneuma, the Spirit, came how everything was changed because they were changed. So Pentecost became a dividing line: on one side spiritual weakness, hesitancy, fear and defeat, and on the other, strength, confidence, courage and victory. However we interpret or explain Pentecost, there is no doubt that it effected a radical change in the experience of the disciples.

Is Pentecost repeatable today? The answer seems to be both 'yes' and 'no'. If we ask, 'can Pentecost be reproduced in its original form? The answer is 'no'. It was a 'one-off', extraordinary, foundational experience, which some have called the birthday of the Church. But what of the inner experience the disciples knew? The fact is that while there were some external miracles associated with Pentecost, the greatest miracle was not in the external phenomena, but in the hearts of these men and women. Now we can claim all that Christ died for, including the Spirit's fullness. – LE

A prayer:

Breathe on me, breath of God,
Fill me with life anew,
That I may love what Thou dost love,
And do what Thou wouldst do.

Edwin Hatch (1835 – 89)

THE HIGH COST OF LOW LIVING

You have sown much, and bring in little; you eat, but do not have enough; you drink, but you are not filled with drink; you clothe yourselves, but no one is warm; and he who earns wages, earns wages to put into a bag with holes (Haggai 1: 6).

With these words the prophet is spelling out to the people something that sounds very familiar to modern ears. For all their strivings and endeavours the people were finding no satisfaction, and their money disappeared 'like flour through a sieve'. This was God's way of speaking to the people of that day through circumstances such as rising prices and inflation.

The burden of Haggai's prophecy was to protest against the godlessness of his people, who, after their restoration, had allowed the Temple to remain in ruins. We can feel the anger and the indignation of the prophet as he contrasted his countrymen's concern for themselves over against their contempt of God. They were building their own houses, and dwelling at ease in them, while the House of the Lord stood in ruins. With painful effect Haggai uses the selfishness of his people as a rod with which to beat them.

What had they gained by seeking self at the expense of God? Nothing had prospered with them. Instead of cheating God they had been cheating themselves! The cost of living had gone up. Food and drink and clothing had reached extortionate prices, and money had lost its purchasing power. This kind of scenario is not unknown in our modern world, and it is the biggest economic problem for many countries right now. It is interesting how Haggai makes a connection between economic problems and the people's attitude to God. The neglected Temple was a patent symbol of their moral and spiritual condition. The abiding principle emerges that to neglect God is to pay a high price. There is a link between a nation's well-being and its attitude to God and His laws.

It is for this reason that we need to pray for our nation. We need leaders with spiritual vision, those who see beyond economic factors, political expediency and materialistic aspirations. Only a return to God and His laws can save us. – LE

A prayer:
Lord, your Word exhorts us to pray for all in authority. We lift up the leaders of the nation and ask that they may turn to you for wisdom and direction. Amen.

EARTHEN VESSELS

Each of you should know how to possess his own vessel in sanctification and honour (1 Thessalonians 4: 4).

The life of sanctification and honour is dependent upon our relationship with the Lord Himself. It has to be a relationship in which the Lord Himself is supreme. It is a relationship in which the Lord who dwells within is more important and more manifest than the earthen vessel.

The writer to the Hebrews tells us that all things connected with our life are naked and open unto Him with whom we have to do. Our life also needs to be open to the world so that the light that is within can shine out and so that the treasure that is within the vessel may be seen. In other words, our life is to be open so that the world may see and know that "it is no more I, but Christ who lives in me."

When Paul wrote to Timothy he drew a comparison between the various kinds of vessels that there were in a great house. "In a great house there are not only vessels of gold and silver, but also of wood and of earth; and some to honour, and some to dishonour. If a man therefore purge himself from these, he shall be a vessel unto honour, sanctified, and meet for the master's use" (2 Timothy 2: 20,21). If I may use the same illustration to draw a comparison between a brown earthen vessel and one that is made of glass, we cannot see what is inside an earthen vessel except from one angle, but from every angle we can see what is inside a glass jug.

Our life in its initial stages was very much like an earthen vessel. Then Jesus met with us and saved us by His grace. As we were led on by the Spirit and came to know Him more intimately we discovered something of what it meant to be sanctified. We discovered that the Lord Himself by His Spirit comes to His temple as we open our being fully to Him. We are sanctified by the Spirit that we might be found unto praise and honour and glory at the appearing of Jesus Christ. We are sanctified by the Spirit that we might come to the fullness of the stature of a perfect man in Jesus Christ. – JAH

A prayer:

Live out Thy life within me,
O Jesus, King of kings,
Be Thou Thyself the answer
To all my questionings.
Live out Thy life within me,
In all things have Thy way,
I, the transparent medium,
Thy glory to display.

Frances Ridley Havergal (1836 – 79)

LIVING OUT OF THE OVERFLOW

They chose Stephen, a man full of faith and the Holy Spirit (Acts 6: 5).

Some years ago, Dr William Stidger, a professor of homiletics, wrote a book for ministers entitled *Living out of the Overflow.* The book was saying that preachers ought never to give the impression that they have few resources, but that, if only time would allow, they could go on for another hour. It was an appeal to develop depth and richness to the preaching ministry.

'Preaching out of the Overflow' – that is a fine phrase, but it could be broadened out to apply to the Christian life generally. The fact is, if we understand the New Testament aright, we are meant to *live* out of the overflow. Jesus spoke of rivers of living water flowing from our inmost beings, and the reference is to the Holy Spirit in our lives. One of our greatest needs is to find adequate spiritual resources to face and overcome all the trials, temptations and pressures of life.

But is it possible that we can be *'full of power'* with resources enough to see us through to victory? One of the outstanding models of this principle was, undoubtedly, Stephen whose story is told in the Acts of the Apostles. When Luke wanted a characteristic word for Stephen he chose *'full'*. When the apostles set out the qualifications for those who were to engage in practical service, they were to be those "known to be full of the Spirit and wisdom" (Acts 6: 3).

However we understand the term, it must be consistent with the *personhood* of the Holy Spirit, so it must have to do with *relationship*. There is a helpful definition in Thayer's *Greek Lexicon:* "What takes possession of the mind is said to fill it." We speak of people being 'filled with fear', 'filled with hate', and so on. To be filled with the Holy Spirit means that we have come under His control. This takes out of the imagery the crude literalism of 'fullness' and brings it back to where all Christian experience finds its centre – in relationships. It is when I rightly relate to the Holy Spirit that I can experience living out of the overflow.

Thomas Cook, author of *New Testament Holiness,* said: "Pentecost is God's coronation gift that He gives to those who crown Jesus King." – LE

A prayer:

Filled with the Holy Ghost,
Saved to the uttermost,
In Christ alone I'll boast
And forward go.

Anon

AFTER EASTER – WHAT?

We are His witnesses to these things, and so also is the Holy Spirit whom God has given to those who obey Him (Acts 5: 32).

In the early part of the twentieth century, Dr J.D. Jones wrote: "There are two things vital to the very existence of the Church: Easter and Pentecost. Easter gave the Church its gospel; Pentecost gave its power." Is it possible that in experience we may be living between Easter and Pentecost? We have come to know the salvation Christ died and rose again to make possible for us – forgiveness, new life, peace with God – but we have not moved on to claim all that Christ makes possible in the gift of the Holy Spirit.

There is no more important question for the Christian than 'Is there still something more for me, some deeper, fuller work of the Spirit in my life?' We can, of course, close our minds even to the possibility of a deeper work of God, as the dispensationalists do, believing that Pentecost was a 'one-off', never-to-be repeated foundational church experience, or we can ask 'Is what happened to those first disciples of Jesus possible for me today?'

Some argue that they received everything at conversion. If such are assured that they are living in the fullness of the life that Jesus offers to His people, praise God for it! But if there is an awareness of a lack in their spiritual lives then it is time to look at what Jesus promised and prayed for in the experience of Pentecost.

In the earlier days of the Church, the period between Ascension Day and Pentecost was known as 'Expectation Week', and for ten days the disciples waited in obedience to the command of Christ. This is a key factor: the Holy Spirit filled the hearts of *obedient* men and women and it can never be any different for us. The place of obedience is the place of blessing. – LE

A prayer:

Lord, we believe to us and ours,
The apostolic promise given:
We wait the Pentecostal showers,
The Holy Ghost sent down from Heaven.

Charles Wesley (1707 – 88)

THE VERGE OF JORDAN

So the priests who bore the ark stood in the midst of the Jordan until everything was finished that the Lord had commanded Joshua to speak to the people, according to all that Moses had commanded Joshua; and the people hurried and crossed over. Then it came to pass, when all the people were completely crossed over, that the ark of the Lord and the priests crossed over in the presence of the people (Joshua 4: 10, 11).

The children of Israel were faced with a cross-roads experience, literally. The years of wilderness experience was at an end. The Promised Land lay within sight. The only obstacle that now lay before them was the river Jordan. But there was a problem, the river was in full flood (3: 15), overflowing its banks. The rush of water carried all before it. There was no way over. Yet the command to Joshua was plain: "arise, go over this Jordan, thou and all the people" (1: 2, *AV*). How was it to happen? Surely the answer was simple! It had happened before. Admittedly only Joshua and Caleb could remember it, everyone else of that generation was dead. But everyone knew the formula. Joshua would lift up the rod, stretch out his hand and the waters would divide. Not this time! It was as if God said: 'You know what I have been able to do in the past, now you have to trust that I can do it again.'

The command was for the priests to take the Ark of the Covenant, the symbol of God's presence with His people, and step out into the flood water. Not until the *soles of the feet* of the priests were in the flood water would the dry path appear. The command was to shoulder the responsibility of the Presence of the Lord, step out on His promise, even though the way ahead seemed impossible.

What is needed to meet the need in today's church is people prepared to take upon themselves the name of the Lord, shoulder the responsibility of His Presence, step out on His promise into the worldliness that threatens to sweep all before it, and STAND FIRM until all have crossed from the wilderness of Sin to the land of Promise. – DD

A prayer:
Lord, I no more Thy truth blaspheme, Thy truth I lovingly receive; I can, I do believe in Thee; all things are possible to me. Amen. - Charles Wesley (1707 – 88)

VALLEY OF DRY BONES

I will pour water on him who is thirsty, and floods on the dry ground (Isaiah 44: 3).

Ezekiel's vision of the valley of dry bones is, sadly, so often a picture of the churches. James A. Stewart, in *Come Breath,* makes the observation: "The Lord set Ezekiel down in the midst of the valley of dry bones. Many Christian workers believe that the Lord has done the same thing for them! They have been called to be the Lord's messengers to dry bones. How many dear pastors are preaching to congregations Sunday after Sunday with no apparent sign of life."

We need to remind ourselves what Jesus promised when He spoke of the Spirit's coming. Whatever else we may make of His words, one thing we can say: no one can remain spiritually dry having once received the experience set forth by our Lord. In John's Gospel we have the challenging words of Jesus: "If anyone is thirsty, let him come to Me and drink. He who believes in Me, as the Scripture has said, out of his heart will flow rivers of living water" (John 7: 37,38).

John adds: "But this He spoke concerning the Spirit, whom those believing in Him would receive; for the Holy Spirit was not yet given, because Jesus was not yet glorified" (verse 39). Those believers were to enter into a new relationship which would bring spiritual fullness, new resources, new power, an overflowing experience that could only be described by the metaphor 'rivers of living water' flowing from within. But there is a condition: "If anyone thirsts ..." It is a big IF. Is it not true that our biggest problem is that often we are not thirsty enough? We thirst for many things: success, money, things, for human love, approval, recognition, applause, but we do not thirst for God.

In recent years, the country has gone through severe drought conditions and much concern has been expressed about it. The church needs to be concerned about spiritual dryness and begin to seek the Lord in earnest prayer. – LE

A prayer:
The cleansing stream I see, I see! I plunge, and oh, it cleanseth me! Oh, praise the Lord! It cleanseth me, it cleanseth me, yes, cleanseth me. - Phoebe Palmer (1807 - 1887)

DARE TO BE DIFFERENT

Having these promises, beloved, let us cleanse ourselves from all filthiness of the flesh and spirit, perfecting holiness in the fear of God (2 Corinthians 7: 1).

One of the greatest challenges to Christian living is the tension of living a life of holiness in a very unholy world, of being pure in the midst of all kinds of polluting influences. John Blanchard in *What in the World is a Christian?* makes the point that we must live as Christians, not in the world as we would like it to be, but in the world as it is.

Of course, Christians of every age have had to wrestle with the same problem. The New Testament shows that the world has never been a friend to grace, and frequently demonstrates the difficulty of living a holy life in an unholy, alien, hostile and unsympathetic world. In some respects evil is more aggressive, persuasive, and more invasive today than in the past generations. The media has radically altered the accepted 'norms' of morality and has exerted a strong influence on the patterns of human behaviour.

But if we accept the Bible as the unchanging Word of God in which God's pattern for living is laid down, then we are called upon to resist all these pressures and be true to our calling as the people of God. One of the important biblical truths related to this problem is the concept of separation. Paul writes clearly about the distinctive nature of the Christian and the need to be different. '"Come out from among them and be separate," says the Lord' (2 Corinthians 6: 17) is a word, not of cold legalism but is born of love and concern (2 Corinthians 6: 16 and 18).

Dr James Denney, a Scottish theologian, said: "There is no conception of holiness in the Bible into which the idea of separation does not enter." The power and authority of the church depends upon its daring to be different. As Christians we must ever keep in our sights the distinctive nature of the life to which we are called. Christian 'apartness' is a quality of life, a call to be salt and light in the world. God's call to holiness is not legalistic, cold and austere, it is so that the most intimate fellowship with God becomes possible. – LE

A prayer:
I delight to do your will, O my God, and your law is in my heart (Psalm 40: 8).

PRAYER THAT TRANSFORMS

As He prayed, the appearance of His face was altered (Luke 9: 29).

The New Testament records that when Jesus took with Him Peter, James and John onto the mountain to pray, He was transfigured before them. Prayer has a transforming power! On that particular occasion it was a change in the physical appearance of Jesus. But the text is symbolic of the wider truth that prayer has transforming power in our lives, in the Church, and in the world.

We say 'prayer changes things', but do we really believe it? There can be no doubt that there is a desperate need for change in the churches and in the world, and only God can effect that change! But the Bible shows, and history confirms, that God works as His people pray. We don't have to understand all the 'why's' and 'wherefore's' but we do need to believe the fact.

J. Ithel Jones points out that the New Testament teaches that there are certain unmistakable qualities in the life of the Church when it lives in the power of the Holy Spirit, which are conspicuously absent from the life of the Church today. One such quality is a vigorous corporate prayer life. These people believe in prayer and especially in the prayer of God's people in concert. They would allow nothing to interfere with this strong prayer life. In Acts 6 we read of the Church's need for organisation. Trouble had arisen over the Poor Fund, and so the apostles decided to set up a committee to administer the fund so that the work of prayer and the ministry of the Word might not be hindered.

That is rather interesting! The purpose of the first committee formed in the Church was to attend to the subsidiary matters so that the hands of the leaders might be free to attend to first priorities. The Early Church was an organised and a praying church but with this emphasis: *it was organised in order that it might give itself more thoroughly to prayer.*

Can we imagine what would happen to the Christian cause in Britain if every church called its people to earnest prayer as a first priority? – LE

A prayer:
Lord, we cannot do your work in our own strength, we know it is time to seek the Lord. Keep us faithful at the throne of grace, we pray. Amen.

IF MY PEOPLE ...

If My people who are called by My name will humble themselves, and pray and seek My face, and turn from their wicked ways, then I will hear from heaven, and will forgive their sin and heal their land (2 Chronicles 7: 14).

What a promise God has given us! It is worth asking some questions concerning it.

Why do we need revival?

"If my people..." When God made His promise to Solomon that He would heal the land, the fulfilment was dependent on those who were called by His name humbling themselves before Him in repentance. God always starts revival with His own people. So do we need reviving today? We are living in an age when evil confronts us on every side.

If we acknowledge Christ as our Lord and Saviour, are our lives a rebuke to those who indulge in sin, those who have no thought of Him? Is the Holy Spirit having His way in us so that the 'rivers of living water' flow through us, creating in others a thirst for Him? Are we a people who daily delight to do His will, or are we going through the motions of worship with little thought to His claims on our lives, and of the need of lost souls around us? *If the preaching of the Word of God is not bearing fruit in our lives, we are in desperate need of revival!*

Jesus said: "Without Me you can do nothing" (John 15: 5). How slow we are to learn this lesson. We fail to open our hearts fully to the indwelling presence of the Holy Spirit, and then wonder why we make so little impact on the world around us.

What revival is not

Revival could hardly come without our emotions being stirred, but emotional experiences are not revival. It cannot be worked up, it is sent down from Heaven. Revival is not enthusiasm for the work of God and it is not all-out evangelism, or seeing many of those without Christ brought to Him. These things will be the outcome of revival, but they are not revival in themselves. Neither is revival the witnessing of miracles or gifts bestowed upon the church of God. *Revival starts in the heart.* – JG

A prayer:
Revive Thy work, O Lord, Thy mighty arm make bare; speak with the voice that wakes the dead, and make Thy people hear. Amen. - Albert Midlane (1825 – 1909)

A NEW DISCOVERY OF JESUS

I am the vine, you are the branches. He who abides in Me, and I in him, bears much fruit; for without Me you can do nothing (John 15: 5).

Professor James S. Stewart said: "Revival is a new discovery of Jesus." According to the Rev Duncan Campbell, one of the outstanding characteristics of the Lewis Awakening of 1949-53 was an awareness of God. That awareness always brings with it an awesome sense of God's holiness, till with Isaiah we cry: "... I am undone ... I am a man of unclean lips ... For my eyes have seen the King, the Lord of hosts" (6: 5). That awareness of God is invariably accompanied by a deep conviction of sin, causing God's people to reach out to Him in repentance and for cleansing and a renewed relationship with Him.

And when God touches His people in this way, the awareness of Him spreads into the local area, sometimes over a nation and even abroad. To quote Duncan Campbell again: "I have no hesitation in saying that this awareness of God is the crying need of the Church today." Revival is the waking out of spiritual sleep to 'a new discovery of Jesus', bringing with it a passionate love for Him and for souls, a hunger for the Word of God and for prayer.

Revival brings a right relationship with God, but it also involves having a right relationship with others. I heard recently of a woman who had harboured bitter resentment for years against her former pastor. She was crippled with rheumatoid arthritis, but God spoke to her about her bitterness. She repented and apologised to the pastor and was immediately healed. If a wrong relationship with others can so affect our physical health, how much more will it affect our spiritual health. A right relationship with both God and others is surely a first step towards revival.

Behind every revival there is a praying people. But prayer must be accompanied by obedience. Are we willing to pay the price of humbling ourselves before Him in obedience and prayer? Surely the cost can never be too great in the light of Calvary. – JG

A prayer:
Revive Thy work, O Lord, create soul-thirst for Thee; and hungering for the bread of life, O may our spirits be! Amen. - Albert Midlane (1825 – 1909)

THE SALTY TANG OF SAINTLINESS

You are the salt of the earth; but if the salt loses its flavour, how shall it be seasoned? It is good for nothing but to be thrown out and trampled under foot by men (Matthew 5: 13).

"You are the salt of the earth." So life without Christ is unbearably insipid. It is only with Him that we keep what Oswald Chambers called 'the salty tang of saintliness'. Salt preserves wholesomeness and prevents decay. It makes you wonder, doesn't it, what would happen to modern society with all its moral rottenness if it were not for the presence of the Christian Church.

Talking of salt, I have recently read *Pride and Perjury*, the autobiographical book by Jonathan Aitken, the former government minister. Having been found guilty of perjury, he reflects on the inevitable prison sentence he was about to receive. Awaiting sentence, he visited Sandwich Bay, Kent, rising early each morning to walk by the sea, to ponder and pray. It occurred to him that there is something about the combination of sea and stillness which stirred his soul.

He recalled that many years before a science teacher told him that there is precisely the same percentage of salt in a drop of sea-water as there is in a drop of human blood. Ever since absorbing that 'biological revelation' (accurate or not) he said he had instinctively felt that going down to the sea can be a return to the roots of our being and a renewal of the spirit and substance of which we are made. It is an interesting observation. Certainly it was by the sea that the battered and beaten Simon Peter was restored to full fellowship with his Lord and not long afterwards, filled with the Holy Spirit, was proclaiming the gospel with outstanding results.

Oswald Chambers remarked that our Lord used in illustration the most conspicuous things known, i.e. salt, light, a city on a hill. He said that it is a 'disadvantage' to be salt (and light) precisely because it means being exposed! Our confession of Jesus Christ cannot be a secret thing, but gloriously public. – NA

A prayer:
Dear Father God, help us to so live as salt and light amidst the corruption of this world that our lives may be a wholesome influence to point others to the truth as it is in Jesus.

64

THE BODY OF CHRIST

By one Spirit we were all baptized into one body (1 Corinthians 12: 13).

After Christ came, faith was exercised not in regard to a coming Christ, although He is coming again, but in a Christ who *has come*. But in both cases it meant war against the devil, and the claim to liberty from the devil's thrall; liberty to praise and serve God.

When Christ came, incarnate in the flesh – that is to say, came in the form of a human body – He lived, suffered, died, rose again and ascended. Then He poured out the Holy Spirit. On the night of the resurrection the risen Christ came and breathed upon His disciples and they received the Spirit of God, the Spirit of life. But at Pentecost the Spirit of God came not only into men but upon men. Then began the greatest work of all, the preparation of the Body of Christ. Christ's Body is the Church, the kingly body which is again to reign upon this earth ... [that is], the Body of Christ will be made up of those who are "baptized by one Spirit into one body," the holy and the pure (1 Corinthians 12: 13).

Satan is wounded but still makes war upon the Body of Christ. He is not yet bound, he knows that his time is short, and consequently he is tremendously active. These are battle days, and they ought to be triumph days. If God contended with Satan about the body of Moses, will He not contend with Satan about the Body of Christ?
Of course He will. – RH

A prayer:

O that all with us might prove,
The fellowship of saints!
Find supplied, in Jesus' love,
What every member wants:
Grasp we our high calling's prize,
Feel on earth our sins forgiven,
Rise, in His whole image rise,
And meet our Head in heaven!

THE BODY OF SIN

Knowing this, that our old man was crucified with Him, that the body of sin might be done away with, that we should no longer be slaves to sin (Romans 6: 6).

"That the body of sin might be destroyed." So what is the meaning of the expression 'the body of sin'? The word 'body' is used by St Paul in three senses. Firstly, the mortal body of flesh and blood and bones. When this meaning of the word is intended in Scripture it is plainly shown by the context, such as "glorify God in your body." In cases where it might be misunderstood the word 'mortal' is put before it. "Let not sin reign in your mortal body" (Romans 6: 12). The word 'mortal' does not appear in our text. It is significantly absent. Therefore the mortal body is not referred to.

If additional proof were needed to show that the mortal body is not referred to, it would be found in the fact, first, that sin is not in matter – not in flesh and blood – but as our Lord said, it is *in the heart;* that is, in the mind, appetites, and will, and secondly, that the mortal bodies of God's faithful people are not destroyed as a condition precedent to serving not sin, but God.

Secondly, the body of Christ. Here the word 'body' is used in a mystical sense as referring to the Church, and is, of course, not referred to in our text. Thirdly, the body of sin. Here the word 'body' is again used in a mystical sense, as referring to indwelling sin, a principle enslaving the mind, appetites and will. This is undoubtedly the meaning of the word in our text as the context clearly affirms: "That the body of sin might be destroyed, that henceforth we should not serve sin."

Our text therefore declares that through the crucifixion of "our old man," by virtue of our complete identification with Christ on the Cross, we may claim that the body of sin – the principle of sin – may be destroyed, done away. Radical destruction was undoubtedly St Paul's idea in using the word in our text. – RH

A prayer:

> *Come, Saviour, come and make me whole,*
> *Entirely all my sins remove;*
> *To perfect health restore my soul,*
> *To perfect holiness and love.*

Charles Wesley (1707 – 88)

AN UTTERMOST SAVIOUR

Having been set free from sin, and having become slaves of God, you have your fruit to holiness, and the end, everlasting life (Romans 6: 22).

Romans 6 is one of the great passages upon which Wesley based his teaching of deliverance from indwelling sin. All out-and-out teachers of scriptural holiness accept this view. Should there, however, remain a doubt in any honest mind as to whether 'the body of sin' refers to the mortal body or to the enslaving principle of indwelling sin, let that honest mind ask itself which rendering of the text will glorify God the more. The mortal body theory robs scriptural holiness of one of the strongest proof texts, contradicts the general teaching of Scripture, and postpones real deliverance from sin until after death. While the other rendering once more declares Christ to be an uttermost Saviour, and proclaims to sin-bound humanity a present and complete release from the slavery of sin.

Lastly, let us remember that this experience of complete deliverance from sin in this life by faith in the Lord Jesus Christ, is not a privilege which we can accept or decline, but an obligation. Not to be what we ought to be, what we can be, what God desires us to be, is an offence against God, as well as an injury to our fellowman and ourselves. The present possibility of grace determines the present duty of enjoying it. We are called to live in an age of deep, wide, broad, and insidious Satanic operation. A rising tide of worldliness is sweeping through our churches. Purity of heart is neglected and even disclaimed, while purity in other realms is vehemently insisted on.

All are in favour of pure water, pure food, and even pure drugs. Let us see to it that in the spiritual and eternal realm there shall be purity, and purity God-wrought, by the destruction of the carnal mind, which is enmity against God, and by the enthronement of Christ as the ruling Monarch of our being. – RH

A prayer:

Lord, we Thy presence seek;
May ours this blessing be;
Give us a pure and lowly heart,
A temple meet for Thee.

Attr William J. Hall (1793 – 1861)

THE SERMON ON THE MOUNT

Seeing the multitudes, He went up on a mountain, and when He was seated His disciples came to Him. Then He opened His mouth and taught them (Matthew 5: 1, 2).

The teaching of the Sermon on the Mount is overwhelmingly and disastrously penetrating. Jesus Christ does not simply say, 'thou shalt not do certain things'; He demands that we have such a condition of heart that we never even think of doing them, every thought and imagination of heart and mind is to be unblameable in the sight of God. Who is sufficient for these things: an unsullied purity that never lusts, a forgiving disposition that loves its enemies, a generous spirit that 'taketh not account of evil'? That standard can produce only one thing in an open-eyed man, absolute despair. What is the use of saying, 'all we need is to know what Jesus Christ teaches and then live up to it': where are you going to begin? If we are Christians we have to live according to the teaching of the Sermon on the Mount, and the marvel of Jesus Christ's salvation is that He puts us in the place where we can fulfil all the old law and a great deal more.

Be careful not to be caught up in the clap-trap of today which says, 'I believe in the teachings of Jesus, but I don't see any need for the Atonement.' Men talk pleasant, patronizing things about Jesus Christ's teaching while they ignore His Cross. By all means let us study Christ's teaching, we do not think nearly enough along New Testament lines, we are swamped by pagan standards, and as Christians we ought to allow Jesus Christ's principles to work out in our brains as well as our lives, but the teaching of Jesus apart from His Atonement simply adds an ideal that leads to despair.

What is the good of telling me that only the pure in heart can see God when I am impure? Of telling me to love my enemies when I hate them? I may keep it down but the spirit is there. Does Jesus Christ make it easier? He makes it a hundredfold more difficult! The purity God demands is impossible unless we can be re-made from within, and that is what Jesus Christ undertakes through the Atonement. He came to *make* us what He teaches we should be, that is the difference. – OC

A prayer:

O God, Father of our Lord Jesus Christ, you are holy and cannot look upon sin, yet I am sinful. I long to be clean and I come to the Cross for cleansing. Create in me a clean heart, O God, and renew a right spirit in me. For your name's sake. Amen.

THE PASSIONATE FEW

Where two or three are gathered in My name, I am there in the midst of them (Matthew 18: 20).

The Passionate Few is the title of an essay by F.W. Boreham. In it he asks the question: "Why is it that great literature survives? The average man cares little or nothing for Shakespeare. The answer is: the fame of classical authors is made and maintained by 'the passionate few'." So everything depends on the passionate few. And on the human level, the Christian cause depends so much on the passionate few – those who believe and pray and serve passionately.

In every congregation of the Church there might be what Spener called an *ecclesiola in ecclesia* – 'a little church with the church' – or, as we have already described it, 'the passionate few'. This is not to encourage the idea of any spiritually superior clique, but it is to face the realistic fact that real intercessors have always been in the minority in the Church, and it is still so today.

As far as we know, the disciples asked Jesus to teach them only one thing, that is, to pray. The Church in every generation has needed to be taught to pray, to learn the lesson that God's purposes can be achieved only through God's power, and that power can come in no other way than through prayer. The pray-er is always saying one thing to God: "Lord, we need you! We cannot do your work in our own strength."

There is in Britain today a dearth of real intercessors – those who know how to lay hold of the promises of God, to claim victories in Christ's name, to touch the throne of God in fervent, believing prayer. No movement can ever be outdated or irrelevant which seeks to move in line with God's unchanging purpose for His people and the world. And for the churches today, what could be more urgent than to seek God for the infilling of the Holy Spirit for all believers, for the spread of scriptural holiness and the revival of the Church?

The passionate few long that others will share their concern and join with them for revival today. – LE

A prayer:
"O God, if still the holy place is found of those in prayer, by all the promises of grace I claim an entrance there" - Albert Orsborn (1886 – 1967)

WHEN THE GILT WEARS OFF

Those who wait on the Lord shall renew their strength; they shall mount up with wings like eagles, they shall run and not be weary, they shall walk and not faint (Isaiah 40: 31).

In his essay *The Tireless Trudge*, F.W. Boreham asks: "Which is the most trying part of a long journey to be undertaken on foot?" Is it the beginning with the long road stretching out interminably before you? Or is it the final stage where, exhausted, you are hardly able to put one foot in front of the other? Boreham argues neither! Rather there is a certain exhilaration in starting a new venture, and the final goal in sight draws forth renewed effort. But what about the intermediate stage – the long middle stretch? This, says Boreham, is the worst and most difficult part of the journey. This is precisely what Isaiah meant in the quotation above.

We can imagine those pilgrims setting off with enthusiasm, and of seeing Jerusalem at last in sight: mounting up with wings as eagles at the beginning, overcoming tiredness by the sight of the city and running without being weary. But Isaiah is thinking of the long middle stretch – the drag across the desert. Boreham has a gem of a sentence: *Grace holds on when the gilt wears off.*

In all Christian work we have to learn this lesson. It is not easy to keep going when little seems to happen, when the initial excitement of a new venture has worn off and the goal of achievement lies still beyond the horizon of our vision. Such commitment seems rare these days. So often churches seem to change rapidly from one fad to another, ringing the changes in a desperate effort to fill the emptiness of so much of our living.

The great need is to identify the priorities of prayer, of obedience to God's unchanging truth, of steady commitment to Christ's will and purpose for His people. It does take a special grace to do this and to keep going when there is little to encourage us. But this is the only way to arrive at God-appointed goals. Those who continue faithfully, patiently and hopefully will be surprised at the times of refreshing from the Lord which they would have missed had they left in the hour of discouragement. – LE

A prayer:

Have Thine own way, Lord, have Thine own way; hold o'er my being absolute sway. Amen. – Adelaide A. Pollard (1862 – 1934)

THE GLORIOUS PROMISE

"Bring all the tithes into the storehouse, that there may be food in My house, and try me now," says the Lord of hosts, "if I will not open for you the windows of heaven and pour out for you such a blessing that there will not be room enough to receive it" (Malachi 3: 10).

We have in this prophecy a graphic picture of the closing period of the age. It is a picture which has a dark side. On the dark side we have portrayed the sins of a dishonest, ungrateful people, and an unfaithful priesthood. Blemished offerings were brought to the altar for sacrifice; treacherous dealings in business with one another; impurity in social life; mixed marriages with the heathen and divorce running like a prairie fire through the land. Tithes belonging to God were selfishly withheld. They were dishonouring God and honouring sinners.

On the bright side there is the glorious promise of the coming Messiah, the dawning of a new day, and the presence of the mysterious figure, 'the Messenger of the Covenant'.

As we hold this in mind, let us compare it with our own times. We are living in the END days of a great age, and we, too, could paint a very dark picture embracing all the evils that Malachi speaks of. But we, too, are looking for the appearing of the great God and our Saviour Jesus Christ. We also are expecting the latter rain of promise: an outpouring of the Spirit on all flesh, and we also have in our midst the Messenger of the Covenant, the Holy Spirit.

Notice that right in the midst of all this darkness, depression and God-forsaking living, God promises His people *an uncontainable blessing* (3: 10). We have many blessings from God, and we praise Him from whom all blessings flow, but they are all containable. But have we had the blessing that we cannot contain, that is bigger than our capacity? Something that we cannot keep to ourselves? (John 7: 37-39).

Have we the uncontrollable blessing? Something that channels its way through into the thirsty places of other lives? The price is *bring ALL...* - LE

A prayer:

Lord Jesus, may I ever drink of the Living Water. And make me a channel of blessing to the dry and thirsty souls around me. Fill me to overflowing, I pray. Amen.

THE PRESENT MOMENT

Then He spoke a parable to them, that men always ought to pray and not lose heart (Luke 18: 1).

Reflecting on the swift passage of time, is it not the case that so much of life can be lost simply by the habit of always looking into the future. It is as though we are so busy looking forward that we fail to see the preciousness of the present; we are so absorbed with the destination that we fail to enjoy the passing scenery. We all know people who are so busy making a living that they have no time to really live.

This reflection on losing the present has wide implications. When we think of our Christian lives, with the great need for prayer, for holy living, for faithful service, for sacrificial giving, is it not true that so often we push these vital issues into the future – some day but not now! And all the time life moves on and the present is lost.

Equally, as we grow older, we can be forever looking back over the road we have travelled and fail to see what is at hand today. Real usefulness to God means taking hold of the present moment, seeing its value and making it count. There is a *present* need, especially for faithful intercessors. No one, unless totally devoid of spiritual sensitivity, can deny that our greatest need today is for God to come and work in a new way in His Church in Britain. We need those who can pray *now!*

> *O members of the body of Christ, O ye Church of the living God,*
> *O editors, and leaders, and pastors, O saints where our fathers trod:*
> *The voice still insistently whispers; "Answer not, tomorrow I'll pray."*
> *The voice is one of authority – The Church needs reviving today!*

This verse appears in a booklet called *The Royal Exchange* by E.F. and L. Harvey. – LE

A prayer:
To serve the present age, my calling to fulfil, O may it all my powers engage, to do my Master's will! - Charles Wesley (1707 – 88)

THE PROMISE OF REVIVAL

When the enemy comes in like a flood, the Spirit of the Lord will lift up a standard against him. The Redeemer will come to Zion (Isaiah 59: 19, 20).

For months Evan Roberts was hungering after God and His holiness. He came to the point of desperation and brokenness. God met with him and filled him with the Holy Spirit, giving him a vision of coming revival in his beloved Wales. What followed is now history. Going to his home town of Loughor, not far from Swansea, he began with a children's meeting, and soon all Wales was ablaze. What God did in 1904 He can do today.

We must not expect the coming revival to save our dying civilisation, now so near its end. The Acts 2 revival at Pentecost did not save Jerusalem or the Jewish nation from destruction in AD70. But we may believe that it postponed judgment on the doomed city and nation, thus allowing Jewish believers to proclaim the gospel throughout the Roman Empire, and beyond, during the intervening period.

The purpose of revival is not to save civilisation or systems, but to save souls. Paul did not attempt to save a doomed ship, but he was used of God to save those who journeyed with him. Christians today should not give time and energy to political debate or to dying systems, but rather should they seek to save lost souls and to promote spiritual revival.

There are definite promises in the Bible relating to revival before our Lord's return. In Isaiah 59: 19, 20, we read: "When the enemy shall come in like a flood, the Spirit of the Lord shall lift up a standard against him, and the Redeemer shall come to Zion." In Daniel 12: 10, we read (referring to the time of the end): "Many shall be purified and made white." Surely it will take a revival to bring *many* believers into a state of purity and holiness. Joel 2: 23 refers to the promise of the 'early and latter rain', suggesting that the church age will begin and end with revival. – AS

A prayer:

O send another Pentecost,
Thou Lamb for sinners slain;
Quicken Thy saints, bring home the lost,
Revive Thy work again.

THE BURNING HEART

Did not our heart burn within us while He talked with us on the road, and while He opened the Scriptures to us? (Luke 24:32).

We need to learn this secret of the burning heart. Suddenly Jesus appears to us, fires are set ablaze, and we are given wonderful visions; but then we must learn to maintain the secret of the burning heart – a heart that can go through anything. It is the simple, dreary day, with its commonplace duties and people, which smothers the burning heart, unless we learn the secret of abiding in Jesus.

Much of the distress we experience as Christians comes not as a result of sin, but because we are ignorant of the laws of our own nature. For instance, the only test we should use to determine whether or not to allow a particular emotion to run its course in our lives is to examine what the final outcome of the emotion will be. Think it through to its logical conclusion, and if the outcome is something that God would condemn, put a stop to it immediately. But if it is an emotion that has been kindled by the Spirit of God and you don't allow it to have its way in your life, it will cause a reaction on a lower level than God intended.

That is the way unrealistic and overly emotional people are made. And if it is not exercised on its intended level, the higher the emotion, the deeper the level of corruption. If the Spirit of God has stirred you, make as many of your decisions as possible irrevocable, and let the consequences be what they will. We cannot stay forever on the mount of transfiguration, basking in the light of the mountaintop experience (Mark 9: 1-9). But we must obey the light we received there; we must put it into action. When God gives us a vision, we must transact business with Him at that point, no matter what the cost. – OC.

We cannot kindle when we will
The fire which in the heart resides,
The spirit bloweth and is still,
In mystery our soul abides;
But tasks in hours of insight willed
Can be through hours of gloom fulfilled.

A prayer:
Lord God, kindle a flame of sacred love on the mean altar of my heart. Amen.

ABRAHAM'S LIFE OF FAITH

By faith Abraham obeyed when he was called to go out to the place which he would receive as an inheritance. And he went out, not knowing where he was going (Hebrews 11: 8).

In the Old Testament, a person's relationship with God was seen by the degree of separation in that person's life. This separation is exhibited in the life of Abraham by his separation from his country and his family. When we think of separation today, we do not mean to be literally separated from those family members who do not have a personal relationship with God, but to be separated mentally and morally from their viewpoints. This is what Jesus Christ was referring to in Luke 14: 26.

Living a life of faith means never knowing where you are being led. But it does mean loving and knowing the One who is leading. It is literally a life of faith, not of understanding and reason; a life of knowing Him who calls us to go. Faith is rooted in the knowledge of the Person, and one of the biggest traps we fall into is the belief that if we have faith, God will surely lead us to success in the world.

The final stage in the life of faith is the attainment of character, and we encounter many changes in the process. We feel the presence of God around us when we pray, yet we are only momentarily changed. We tend to keep going back to our everyday ways and the glory vanishes. A life of faith is not a life of one glorious mountaintop experience after another, like soaring on eagles' wings, but a life of day-in and day-out consistency; a life of walking without fainting (see Isaiah 40: 31). It is not even a question of the holiness of sanctification, but of something which comes much farther down the road. It is a faith that has been tried and proved and has withstood the test. Abraham is not a type or an example of the holiness of sanctification, but a type of the life of faith, a faith tested and true, built on the true God. *"Abraham believed God ..."* (Romans 4: 3). – OC.

A prayer:

Give me the faith which can remove
And sink the mountain to a plain;
Give me the childlike praying love
Which longs to build Thy house again;
Thy love let it my heart o'erpower,
And all my simple soul devour.

Charles Wesley (1707 – 88)

A BLESSED AND GLORIOUS REALITY

Be filled [being filled] with the Spirit (Ephesians 5: 18).

This is a command of God as binding as any in the Decalogue, but a command that is today, to a great extent, ignored. Thank God, though, for the signs of revival of the spirit of enquiry all over the world. Thank God for the question, which is agitating the Church today: "Is there a second distinct work of grace after conversion, and if so, what is it?" This is the question of questions. Satan has cheated nine-tenths of God's people out of this great blessing; a blessing that would not only make them happy, but also make them effective for God. I believe it is the will of God that all who know and experience this mighty blessing of the filling of the Holy Spirit should not be slow to declare it.

Some people who do not believe in the possibility of this experience say that we Pentecostal Leaguers are simply deluded people. Well, I would rather be deluded *into* this blessing than deluded out of it. But are we deluded? If we *are* deluded, then there are a good many mighty men of God who have also been labouring under the same delusion in time past. The apostles were deluded, that is quite clear, for if they taught one thing more than another, it was the personality of the Holy Spirit who comes to impart not only life, but life abundant, to perform the second work of grace after regeneration.

The early church, too, was deluded, as well as many saints of God in the ages afterwards. George Fox, John and Charles Wesley, among others, were deluded, and thousands of people since, many of them, thank God, are in our midst today, whose names are, perhaps, better known in heaven than on earth. But I thank God that if this appears to be a delusion, it appears so only to those who have not the light.

To us it is a blessed reality. – RH (*When He Is Come, 1897*).

A prayer:
> *Have Thine own way, Lord, have Thine own way;*
> *Hold o'er my being absolute sway;*
> *Fill with Thy Spirit till all shall see*
> *Christ only, always, living in me.*
> Adelaide A. Pollard (1862 – 1934)

81

GREAT GRACE
Great grace was upon them all (Acts 4: 33).

We hear of the radiation of light and heat, and of the power of electricity. There *is* such a thing as the radiation of the Holy Ghost. What a strange reality there was about these people! They carried conviction, they spoke with assurance, they expected results and saw them. What results do you see in *your* prayer meetings, and in *your* work?

"Great grace was upon them all." The literal Greek of that is: *"Great favour was upon them all."* Great favour with God and with everybody who wanted to glorify Him, but great disfavour with those who did not. Never let us try to please everybody! "Woe unto you, when all men speak well of you!" (Luke 6: 26).

"Great grace," what do these words not contain? "God is able to make all grace abound to every good work" (2 Corinthians 9: 8). Will not that cover your need? "And great grace was upon them *all.*" There were no poor specimens! These men and women were living magnets to draw men not to themselves, but to God. That is why they quickly won the then-known world for Jesus Christ.

The divine order revealed to us in this inspired account is: first, a praying people; then a Spirit-filled people; and, lastly, a witnessing people. That is the need of the world today. Untold possibilities lie right before a praying, a Spirit-filled, and a witnessing people. Ask for the true spirit of prevailing prayer. Prevailing prayer must be inspired in the heart by the Holy Ghost; that is the secret. It begins in the heart. It is not pathos, it is not beautiful phraseology, it is not many things that men admire; but it is the outcome of the secret voice of God in the soul, prompting the heart to ask what God is waiting to give. Is there any business on the earth like this? No, none.

Claim the power that moves the arm that moves the world, and the promise shall be fulfilled in your experience, "nothing shall be impossible unto you." – RH.

A prayer:
Lord, grant me the spirit of prevailing prayer. Cleanse me, and fill me, and use me today. Amen.

PRAYING IN THE HOLY SPIRIT (1)

And when they had prayed, the place where they were assembled together was shaken; and they were all filled with the Holy Spirit, and they spoke the word of God with boldness (Acts 4: 31).

In nothing is the need of the Holy Spirit more manifest than in the exercise of prayer. Prayer is the supply-valve of power and blessing,

> *The Christian's vital breath,*
> *The Christian's native air.*

Prayer, true prayer, is a mystery to those who are not filled with the Spirit. To some it is a labour, to others a form; but to those who know God and follow Him wholly, it is a glorious privilege. Prayer is God and man communing through the Holy Ghost. Prayer bridges the gulf between the finite and the Infinite, between Earth and Heaven. We shall never be the channels of blessing to men that God wants us to be, until we have learned to be the channels to Him and from Him that He desires.

In the fourth chapter of Acts we have a divine report of a Pentecostal prayer meeting. May God the Holy Ghost light up the passage and teach us the true secret and privilege of prayer. The account begins with Peter and John being cast into prison; God delivers them and they go back to their own company and have a wonderful prayer and praise meeting. Especially interesting is this account because it is the first record of a prayer meeting after Pentecost. The people composing it were definitely and really baptized with the Holy Ghost, cleansed from sin, filled with God, and were having great blessings and victories: we find them on their knees.

What were the results of the answer to this prayer? Many of the effects are not mentioned, but some are told us here. "They spake the Word of God with boldness." They used scriptural language; they were not ashamed of it; they claimed results up to scriptural standards, and they were not disappointed. – RH.

A prayer:
Lord, teach us to pray (Luke 11: 1).

PRAYING IN THE HOLY SPIRIT (2)

And when they had prayed, the place where they were assembled together was shaken; and they were all filled with the Holy Spirit, and they spoke the word of God with boldness (Acts 4: 31).

What next? "And the multitude of them that believed were of one heart and of one soul." Here you have true unity. It is union between the individual soul and Christ, and the consequent union with one another. That is what we believe to be the true and only possible reunion that will be seen on earth, not a uniformity of doctrine, or of creed, or of organisation, but a heart union with God, and through God with men.

"Neither said any of them that ought of the things which he possessed was his own." Each individual realised he was a trustee for God and for God's people. The love of property, a very strong love, was conquered by a stronger – the love of God shed abroad in the heart by the Holy Ghost. They realised the tremendous truth that if a man is a Christian, then he is a trustee for God of all he possesses. This makes giving a very different thing from what is was before. In the olden days we gave because people worried us; now we have learned that, as trustees of God, we have to give in a way that will be approved and sanctioned by the Heavenly Court of Chancery.

Next, "they had all things common." That is Christian communism – not compulsory, but spontaneous. It does not mean that you are necessarily to give to every lazy beggar who accosts you, for the Scriptures tell us that if a man will not work neither shall he eat! They had all things common, and they showed a blessed and spontaneous willingness to spend and be spent for the glory of God, and for His people. They manifested true Christian communism! Now the communism of the world is, 'yours is mine'; the communism of Jesus Christ is, 'mine is yours, because mine is God's and you, too, belong to God.'

What follows? "And with great power gave the apostles witness of the resurrection of the Lord Jesus." They lived in the power of His resurrection, and of course they could talk about it. And they radiated the power of the Holy Spirit. – RH.

A prayer:
Lord Jesus, we long for another Pentecostal outpouring. Open our hearts to receive you. Amen.

BY MY SPIRIT ...

"Not by might nor by power, but by My Spirit," says the Lord of hosts (Zechariah 4: 6).

The circumstances of the text are shortly these. Israel is in captivity to Babylon. It is, however, the will of God that Jerusalem shall be restored, the Temple rebuilt, and true worship reinstated, prior to, and in preparation for, the first coming of Christ.

In the third chapter of Zechariah we have an Old Testament lesson concerning the negative side of the baptism of the Holy Ghost – purity – the purity that every child of God should possess. In that chapter we find that wonderful scene where, the veil being drawn aside, we can see God and man, and Satan withstanding them; and we learn that great truth of the human factor, that God uses men to carry blessings to men, and that the enemy of mankind does all he can to withstand Him. Then in the fourth chapter of Zechariah we have the story of the golden candlestick and the two olive trees. Here is pictured the positive side of the baptism of the Holy Ghost, life abundant and continuous power. Together they give us a beautiful Old Testament illustration of the Pentecostal blessing and its purpose – the restoration of the spiritual Jerusalem and the preparation of the people of God for the coming of Jesus Christ. The history of Israel in the Old Testament is the story in type of God's dealings with His church generally, as well as with individuals particularly (1 Corinthians 10: 11).

The period in which you and I are living is strangely like the period in which Zechariah lived. The Church today, to a very great extent, is in captivity to the world. But God seeks to restore His people. God is pouring out His Spirit upon all flesh. And I believe He is seeking that every believer shall be really filled with the Holy Ghost, and that there shall be a great restoration of God's people, in preparation for the second coming of our Lord Jesus Christ. – RH

A prayer:
Restore, O Lord, the honour of your name, in works of sovereign power come shake the Earth again ... Bend us, O Lord, where we are hard and cold, in your refiner's fire come purify the gold. Amen. – Graham Kendrick

DEFINITE IN PRAYER

Whatever things you ask when you pray, believe that you have them, and you will have them (Mark 11: 24).

Another condition: they all prayed for the Holy Ghost in Pentecostal measure. They had had the earnest of the Spirit baptism when Jesus breathed upon them and said: "Receive ye the Holy Ghost." But what they now prayed for was something more, the great predicted outpouring of the Holy Ghost. There is a great value in definiteness in this matter of prayer. Be definite with God, and God will be definite with you. Our Lord Himself said on this particular subject: "What things so ever ye desire, when ye pray, believe that ye receive them, and ye shall have them" (Mark 11: 24, *AV*).

Be definite in prayer to God. How wearisome indefiniteness is! The young woman who stands behind the counter in a draper's shop knows what a nuisance an indefinite purchaser is. She comes and looks at half a dozen articles, and turns every one of them over, but cannot find what she wants. At last she does find what she wants, but she cannot make up her mind to pay the price for it! Oh, let us be business-like with God in this matter. He has paid the price, all we have to do is to "ask and receive." They prayed for the Spirit. What a wonderful and all-embracing character there is in prayer for the Spirit!

Praying for and receiving the Spirit includes all the believer needs. Get filled with the Holy Ghost and everything else follows. – RH.

A prayer:

I want, dear Lord, a heart that's true and clean;
A sunlit heart, with not a cloud between;
A heart like Thine, a heart divine, a heart as white as snow;
On me, dear Lord, a heart like this bestow.

I want, dear Lord, a soul on fire for Thee;
A soul baptized with heavenly energy,
A willing mind, a ready hand, to do whate'er I know,
To spread Thy light wherever I may go.

George Jackson (1866 – 93)

PRAYER WITH FAITH

If you then, being evil, know how to give good gifts to your children, how much more will your heavenly Father give the Holy Spirit to those who ask Him? (Luke 11: 13).

Another characteristic was that they all *believed.* Prayer without faith is a mockery. God gives to every man a measure of faith. They exercised the measure of faith they had, they all believed. Now, there may be some things which may need mighty faith, but this does not. Jesus promised the Holy Spirit without qualification. He says: "If ye then, being evil, know how to give good gifts unto your children: how much more shall your heavenly Father give the Holy Spirit to them that ask him?" (Luke 11: 13). How much more? Exercise the faith you have and God will multiply it by His own.

Again, another characteristic was that they all received the Holy Spirit, women as well as men, the laity as well as the ministry. Not one left out, all were filled, and all may be filled today! What was the result? Jerusalem was turned upside down! May God turn this city upside down!

People often complain of their circumstances. Do you not think the apostles' circumstances were rather difficult? Have you ever thought about Peter's difficulties? Peter had to go to Annas and Caiaphas and tell them that they had crucified the Lord of glory. Peter was in danger of arrest. There was not only the affair with Malchus, but he was charged with stealing the body of Jesus ... Put Peter's difficulties alongside yours and you will find that yours look puny in comparison! They *all* received the Holy Ghost. God had no favourites then; God has no favourites now. All may ask and all may receive. Pentecost is repeatable. The need today is not an opened heaven, but many opened hearts and lips and lives for God to use.

Thank God for the day in which we live: for liberty, for free speech, for the possibility of a worldwide evangelisation. Thank God for it, and also take advantage of it. God wants to use somebody here to start a conflagration. Not the fire of destruction – save the destruction of sin and the works of the devil – but the light and power of the Holy Ghost! – RH.

A prayer:
Lord, stir us and waken us until we see the need around us as you see it and then equip us by your Spirit to be your witnesses and messengers. Amen.

HOW TO SEEK THE BLESSING

Abstain from every form of evil. Now may the God of peace Himself sanctify you completely, and may your whole spirit, soul, and body be preserved blameless at the coming of our Lord Jesus Christ (1 Thessalonians 5: 22, 23).

♦ *How to seek.*

Come to a firm determination to seek until you obtain. It is more important for you to be filled with the Holy Ghost than anything else in the world. Let your resolution be settled, decided and uncompromising. *Separate yourself from all evil.* Get yourself away in heart, in home, in life, and in business. What do you think about? For "as a man thinketh in his heart, so is he." How many men live outwardly moral lives who inwardly cherish evil thoughts!

Separate yourself to God. Let the separation be wholesale as well as in detail. My self, my will, my time, my talents, my tongue, my property, my business, my reputation, my family, my all, to *be* and to *do* anything God requires. *Believe God.* Faith is the immediate condition of the reception of the blessing. Believe that God accepts what you yield to Him – your all. Believe that God does the necessary work in what He receives. Should any difficulty arise, remember that difficulties are sometimes permitted to test our faith. Do not seek the results of faith before you believe, but continue to trust steadfastly in Him who "is able to make all grace abound toward you; that ye, always having all sufficiency in all things, may abound unto every good work" (2 Corinthians 9: 8).

Do not wait for feelings. God's order is always: Fact, Faith, Feelings. Let us not reverse it. Trust the written promise and thank God for its fulfilment, apart from any emotion or experimental knowledge. This will assuredly follow, but generally not until we have honoured God by relying on His faithfulness, without any special manifestation of the blessing we are seeking. *Obey God.* Obey the light you have. Say "Yes" to God at every point. If your all is on the altar it will be easy to say "Yes" and mean it. Obey the light He gives in everything. – RH.

A prayer:

Have Thy way, Lord, have Thy way!
This with all my heart I say:
I'll obey Thee, come what may;
Dear Lord, have Thy way!

Salvation Army Chorus

THE BELIEVER'S MAGNA CARTA

If you then, being evil, know how to give good gifts to your children, how much more will your heavenly Father give the Holy Spirit to those who ask Him! (Luke 11: 13).

This is the Magna Carta of the rights of the believer, in the Holy Ghost. These words were probably the first definite statement of our Lord to His disciples concerning the reception of the Holy Ghost. The text not only declares a right, but tells how that right may be enjoyed. Ask and receive.

The Holy Spirit has a double office to perform. First we are born of the Spirit, under the symbol of living water, then baptized with the Spirit, under the symbol of fire. What are the conditions which those who have received the Spirit in regeneration must fulfil in order to be baptized with the Spirit? To all those who are seeking we would say:

♦ *Do you earnestly desire this blessing?* Although born again have you a sense of depravity within and weakness without? Thank God if it is so, for "blessed are they which do hunger and thirst after righteousness: for they shall be filled" (Matthew 5: 6). God puts the hunger within in order to satisfy it. Make sure your sense of need rests on this scriptural basis; that it is your privilege and your duty to be cleansed from all unrighteousness and to be filled with all the fullness of God. Theology, red-hot from God, is very simple. Don't believe in a theology that needs a senior wrangler to explain it.

♦ *Settle in your mind what you are seeking.* It is not angelic perfection; we shall never be angels, even though certain kinds of friends may assure us that we are! It is not Adamic perfection. We shall never be perfect as Adam was. It is not imputed perfection for character cannot be imputed. You are seeking imparted perfection, the perfection of a perfect God coming into your heart, and enabling you to be men and women, in human bodies, in this everyday world, to perfectly fulfil the object of your creation and redemption, even the glory of God and the salvation of men. – RH.

A prayer:
Lord Jesus, create in me a hunger and a thirst for this blessing, and then enable me to seek until I find that the reason for my creation and redemption may be fulfilled in my life. Amen.

STEPS INTO BLESSING

Whatever things you ask when you pray, believe that you receive them, and you will have them (Mark 11: 24).

There must be:
♦ A steadfast purpose.
♦ A complete separation from the world and the flesh in all their forms.
♦ A wholehearted consecration to God.
♦ A simple faith, independent of feeling.
♦ A continuous, unhesitating obedience to all the known will of God.

Having fulfilled the conditions, do not wait, but "ask and receive." God can work immediately. Trust Him to do so. "Whatsoever things ye desire when ye pray, believe that ye *receive* them and ye shall have them" (Mark 11: 24, *AV*). Not *will* receive, or *may* receive, but *do* receive, and *now*.

We have an infinite God, to know, to possess, to reflect, and to refract. As we walk with Him in the light we shall learn what it is to have our capacities enlarged, our privileges widened, our opportunities extended, and the joy of the Lord increasing every day of our life.
Thus shall we be changed "from glory to glory" by the Spirit of the Lord.

I take the promised Holy Ghost,
I take the power of Pentecost
To fill me to the uttermost,
I take, He undertakes.

RH

A prayer:

I'm Thine, O blessed Jesus,
Washed in Thy precious blood;
Now seal me by Thy Spirit
A sacrifice to God.

Mary D. James

THE LAST GREAT BATTLE

"The nations shall know that I am the Lord," says the Lord God, "when I am hallowed [sanctified] in you before their eyes" (Ezekiel 36: 23).

In order that we may get an idea of the tremendous need of a revival of vital, scriptural, Holy Ghost religion, think, for a moment, of the world around us. Examine the religious condition of the European countries. How poor, how formal, how lifeless! What lack of spiritual cultivation. Disciples of Mahomet [Muhammad], Confucius and of Buddha, are boldly advocating their false religions as superior to Christianity, and well may we tremble to think what may be the result of their missionary efforts. But as Professor Max Muller has said: "Christendom requires not a new religion but a *renewed religion.*" Christendom is to a large extent unchristian and in the sorest need of Holy Ghost revival.

From the international we turn to the national outlook. When Queen Victoria came to the throne, she had 130 million subjects, now 350 million are under British rule – one quarter of the population of the whole globe! These 350 million are made up in this way: fifty million are said to be Christians, sixty million are Mohammedans, and 240 million are yet heathen. Only one-seventh of the King's subjects are even nominal Christians, only one fiftieth are church members, and I cannot tell you the diluted decimal that would represent the out-and-out Christians among them.

Look at England! Look at London! The whole race is in motion somewhere. But where? It needs a mighty filling of the Spirit to direct the individual, to direct the church, to direct the nation, to direct the race God-ward and heavenward. Look at the varied forms of aggressive error amongst us. Look at the false religions around us. Look at the general unrest of nations and individuals. The forces of evil are apparently gathering for the last great battle between the supernatural and natural, between the Christ of God and the christ of men. On which side are we? May God help us! RH (1897).

A prayer:
Lord, open our eyes to the desperate state of our nation and our world, then may your Spirit fill us with compassion and direct our actions that we may meet the challenge of our day. Amen.

HOLINESS

Church of God, beloved and chosen,
Church of God for whom Christ died,
Claim thy gifts and praise the Giver!
Ye are washed and sanctified!
Sanctified by God the Father,
And by Jesus Christ His Son,
And by God the Holy Spirit,
Holy, holy, Three in One.

By His will He sanctifieth,
By the Spirit's power within;
By the loving hand that chasteneth,
Fruits of righteousness to win;
By His truth, and by His promise,
By His word, His gift unpriced,
By His blood, and by our union
With the risen life of Christ.

Holiness by faith in Jesus,
Not by effort of thine own,
Sin's domination crushed and broken,
By the power of grace alone;
God's own holiness within thee,
His own beauty on thy brow,
This shall be thy pilgrim brightness,
This thy blessed portion now.

He will sanctify thee wholly;
Body, spirit, soul shall be
Blameless till thy Saviour's coming
In His glorious majesty:
He hath perfected forever
Those whom He hath sanctified;
Spotless, glorious and holy
Is the Church, His chosen Bride.

Francis Ridley Havergal (1836 – 1879)

SOURCES

League of Prayer Council Minutes

League of Prayer Newsletters

Called to be Saints (Centenary History of the Church of the Nazarene, T.A. Noble and Hugh Rae, Didsbury Press (2006)

www.calvaryholinessmission.co.uk

Richard Reader Harris (1847-1909) – An Assessment of the Life and Influence of a Leader of the Holiness Movement, Geoffrey Norman Fewkes. (A dissertation for the degree of Master of Arts in Theology)

A Man on Fire, The Story of Maynard James by Paul James (Moorleys, 1993).

Also see –

Exploring Christian Holiness, Vol 2, Paul M. Bassett and William M. Greathouse, Beacon Hill Press of Kansas City, 1985

Christian Theology, Volume 2, H. Orton Wiley, Beacon Hill Press of Kansas City, 1952

The Theology of Holiness, Dougan Clark 1893 (Classic Reprints)

The History of The Salvation Army, Vols 1-3, Robert Sandall, Nelson

The Life of William Booth, Harold Begbie, Macmillan, 1920 (abridged edition, 1925)

When the Holy Ghost is Come, Samuel Logan Brengle, Salvationist Publishing and Supplies Ltd

When He is Come, Reader Harris, KC, Pentecostal League, 1930

He Heard from God, E.K. Crossley, Salvationist Publishing and Supplies Ltd, 1959

Drysdale – Prophet of Holiness, Norman Grubb, Lutterworth

Adventures of an Agnostic, M. Hooker, Marshall, Morgan and Scott, 1959

The Pentecostals, W.J. Hollenweger, SCM Press, 1972

David Thomas, David Thomas, International Holiness Mission, 1933

Abandoned to God: Oswald Chambers, David McCasland, Discovery House Publishers, 1993

Moody: a Biography, John Pollock, Baker Books, 1963 (reprinted 1984, 1995)